Communications in Computer and Information Science   **1597**

More information about this series at https://link.springer.com/bookseries/7899

María J. Abásolo ·
Gonzalo F. Olmedo Cifuentes (Eds.)

Applications and Usability of Interactive TV

10th Iberoamerican Conference, jAUTI 2021
Sangolquí, Ecuador, December 2–3, 2021
Revised Selected Papers

 Springer

Editors
María J. Abásolo 🆔
National University of La Plata
La Plata, Argentina

Gonzalo F. Olmedo Cifuentes 🆔
ESPE
Sangolqui, Ecuador

ISSN 1865-0929 ISSN 1865-0937 (electronic)
Communications in Computer and Information Science
ISBN 978-3-031-22209-2 ISBN 978-3-031-22210-8 (eBook)
https://doi.org/10.1007/978-3-031-22210-8

This Springer imprint is published by the registered company Springer Nature Switzerland AG
The registered company address is: Gewerbestrasse 11, 6330 Cham, Switzerland

Preface

The 10th Iberoamerican Conference on Applications and Usability of Interactive TV (jAUTI 2021) was organized by the Department of Electrical, Electronics and Telecommunications and the Smart Systems Research Group WiCOM-Energy of the Universidad de las Fuerzas Armadas ESPE (Ecuador) in conjunction with RedAUTI (The Thematic Network on Applications and Usability of Interactive Digital Television), which consists of 32 research groups from universities in 13 Iberoamerican countries (Argentina, Brazil, Colombia, Costa Rica, Cuba, Chile, Ecuador, España, Guatemala, Perú, Portugal, Uruguay, and Venezuela).

The 10th edition was held during December 2–3, 2021, in an online meeting format due to the context of the COVID-19 pandemic, which did not prevent the gathering of researchers from various universities, specifically from Europe and America, to share their research work.

These proceedings contain nine papers referring to the design, development, and user experience of applications for interactive digital television and related technologies. They were selected from 25 papers received at the event after a XX blind peer-review process; they were later extended and underwent a second peer-review process in which each paper received at least XX reviews.

December 2021

María J. Abásolo
Gonzalo F. Olmedo Cifuentes

Organization

Program Chairs

María José Abásolo   National University of La Plata, Argentina
Gonzalo Fernando Olmedo   University of the Armed Forces ESPE, Ecuador
  Cifuentes

Program Committee

Pedro Almeida	University of Aveiro, Portugal
Valdecir Becker	Federal University of Paraíba, Brazil
Vagner Beserra	University of Tarapacá, Chile
Pedro Beça	University of Aveiro, Portugal
Fernando Boronat	Polytechnic University of Valencia, Spain
José María Buades Rubio	University of the Balearic Islands, Spain
Bernardo Cardoso	University of Aveiro, Portugal
Armando De Giusti	National University of La Plata, Argentina
Jorge Ferraz de Abreu	University of Aveiro, Portugal
Angel García Crespo	University Carlos III of Madrid, Spain
Israel González Carrasco	University Carlos III of Madrid, Spain
Manuel González Hidalgo	University of the Balearic Islands, Spain
Alan Guedes	University College London, UK
Anelise Jantsch	Federal University of Rio Grande do Sul, Brazil
Cristina Manresa Yee	University of the Balearic Islands, Spain
Ramon Mas Sansó	Universitat de les Illes Balears, Spain
Francisco Montero Simarro	University of Castilla-La Mancha, Spain
Rita Oliveira	University of Aveiro, Portugal
Antoni Oliver	University of the Balearic Islands, Spain
Douglas Paredes	University of Los Andres, Venezuela
Joaquín Danilo Pina Amargós	Technological University of Havana "José Antonio Echeverría", Cuba
Alcina Maria Prata	Polytechnic Institute of Setúbal, Portugal
Tânia Ribeiro	University of Aveiro, Portugal
Miguel Angel Rodrigo Alonso	University of Córdoba, Spain
Josemar Rodrigues de Souza	University of Bahia State, Brazil
Gustavo Rossi	National University of La Plata, Argentina
Rita Santos	University of Aveiro, Portugal
Cecilia Sanz	National University of La Plata, Argentina

Telmo Silva   University of Aveiro, Portugal
Raisa Socorro Llanes   Technological University of Havana "José
                                 Antonio Echeverría", Cuba

Contents

Usability and UX

The Importance of Personalization and Household Dynamics for Notifications in the TV Ecosystem

Ana Velhinho[1]([✉])(iD), Juliana Camargo[1](iD), Telmo Silva[1](iD), and Rita Santos[2](iD)

[1] Digimedia, Department of Communication and Arts, University of Aveiro, 3810-193 Aveiro, Portugal
{ana.velhinho,julianacamargo,tsilva}@ua.pt

[2] Digimedia, Águeda School of Technology and Management, University of Aveiro, 3754-909 Aveiro, Portugal
rita.santos@ua.pt

Abstract. Notifications are frequently used in mobile devices and smart environments as a mechanism to deliver personalized messages. However, in the context of the TV ecosystem, notifications are not yet widely used. Hence, this research aims to explore the potential of that context to disseminate important information, recommend content and encourage interactions between individuals. The article presents the results from a survey of studies using notifications, which led to the design of relevant use scenarios focused on the TV. Six thematic scenarios were discussed in a focus group with potential users: 1) CONTENT (TV and over-the-top), 2) SOCIAL (telecommunications and social media), 3) SERVICES (shopping apps and coupons), 4) HEALTH (monitoring and well-being recommendations), 5) CALENDAR (appointments and events), 6) INFO (useful information). The studies from the survey highlighted healthcare alerts, smart home experiences and target advertising as contexts of research. The aim of socialization was addressed in fewer studies but was well received and shown potential. Therefore, one of the scenarios discussed in the focus group included the social dimension. The results shown that focus group participants responded well to general notifications on the TV (e.g. weather, content recommendation and services), whereas shown apprehension regarding personal notifications (e.g. calendar appointments, social media or health alerts), mainly for privacy issues. Nevertheless, they pointed out the scenarios with personal notifications as the most useful for the elderly, which led to a second focus group with this target audience. The insights from this research will allow the development and testing of prototypes in field trials with the support of a Portuguese Pay-TV provider.

Keywords: Notifications · iTV · Focus group · Use scenarios

1 Introduction

Notifications are a mechanism that captures users' attention with the potential to increase the use of digital applications and provide primary and personalized information [1–4].

© Springer Nature Switzerland AG 2022
M. J. Abásolo and G. F. Olmedo Cifuentes (Eds.): jAUTI 2021, CCIS 1597, pp. 3–19, 2022.
https://doi.org/10.1007/978-3-031-22210-8_1

Therefore, notifications are widely adopted in personal mobile devices, however within the TV ecosystem [5] is not as common, probably because the TV is still a device often used collectively. Nevertheless, recent studies have evaluated notification systems in smart environments, including second-screen devices, as means to encourage engagement and connect people [6–8]. To map these contributions, a survey of studies was conducted to identify strategies, critical points and relevant usage scenarios to explore the potential of notifications in the TV ecosystem. Afterwards, one focus group was carried out to discuss about relevant use scenarios to be implemented by a Portuguese Pay-TV provider. Hence, the main goal of this article is to understand, through the analysis of recent studies and feedback from potential users, the receptiveness of notifications in the television ecosystem, namely to content discovery, but also to connect people, delivery useful information, promote local events and foster health and well-being. The document is divided into five sections: Sect. 1, the introduction that presents the scope and objectives of the study; Sect. 2, the contextualization of notifications' mechanism applications; Sect. 3, the methodology that includes the data collection procedures and the sample, respectively of the literature review and of the focus group; Sect. 4, that presents the results and discussion of the two stages of the research aiming to prepare the development and field trials of a prototype; and Sect. 5, the final considerations and future work which point out the insights and challenges on user's preferences and personalization.

2 Paving the Potential of Notifications in the TV Ecosystem

Notifications can facilitate access to priority and updated information by capturing and managing the user's attention about a given subject or content [9]. For this reason, notifications can be a pivotal feature in communication systems, with the potential to be applied to several connected devices, with emphasis on personal mobile devices, such as smartphones [10]. Contexts of use range from personal day-to-day information management to business applications around targeted marketing campaigns. Given the ubiquity and quantity of digital stimuli, it is necessary to assess the most appropriate formats for these notification mechanisms and the receptivity of their use for different contexts, objectives and devices.

Currently, notifications are frequently adopted by smart devices, such as tablets, mobile phones and wearables (e.g., smartwatches and smart glasses). Major industry companies have been investing in the development of Voice User Interfaces (VUIs), which allow using spoken commands to control digital devices [12]. This trend has generalised to using voice assistants to control personal devices and smart environments (e.g., Smart Home). The assistants Alexa, Siri and Google Home, respectively launched by the dominant companies Amazon, Apple and Google, are successful examples of conversational interfaces that explore natural interactions with different devices and include notification mechanisms, namely in the TV context. Nevertheless, notifications are still a relatively rare mechanism and it raises some privacy issues, as TV continues to be used collectively [11]. Despite that, the proliferation of Smart TVs has encouraged a more recurrent use of notifications to alert about new releases as well as measuring users' consumption, mostly focused on over-the-top content delivered by connected media players (e.g. Roku; Apple TV; Android TV, Amazon Fire TV, etc.) and subscription video-on-demand platforms (e.g. Netflix, HBO, Amazon Prime Video, Hulu, etc.).

3 Methodology

3.1 Literature Review

Protocol and Sample Characterization. For the data collection of recent studies assessing contexts, target audiences and guidelines about how notifications can be used in the TV ecosystem, a query[1] on the Scopus and the Web of Science databases was carried out, considering a timeframe from 2015 to the present. Boolean operators AND (to associate the notifications with "TV") and OR (to include similar words in the search) were applied to the following combination of keywords: "notifications", "push notifications", "iTV", "television", "interactive television" and "Smart TV". Because most of the studies about notifications were not oriented to the TV ecosystem, and due to the relevance of older adults regarding the use of the TV at home, the keywords "senior" and "elderly" were adjunct to the search. The results in the Scopus database returned a total of 45 articles, from which 22 were excluded for not fitting into the topic of the study. The query with the same criteria performed in the Web of Science database obtained 14 results, but only 2 were considered for analysis because the others were repeated. Tables 1 and 2 present the sample of 25 articles mapped from both databases. After the analysis of the articles, they were divided into two embracing subject matters identified in the collected studies: notifications for senior audiences regarding remote care and health (Table 1) and notifications' guidelines for the TV ecosystem (Table 2), both detailed in the Results.

Table 1. Notifications for senior audiences regarding remote care and health

Year	Authors of the article	Topic of the study
2020	Macls et al. [13]	Multi-device telecare framework
2019	Corcella et al. [14]	Personalization of remote assistance
2018	Santana-Mancilla and Anido-Rifón [15]	Care system through iTV with health reminders
2018	Silva et al. [16]	Comparative usability study for iTV interface for seniors
2018	Watanapa et al. [17]	Intelligent system to provide assistance when detecting falls
2017	Coelho et al. [6]	Fighting social isolation of older adults with TV, Facebook and multimodality

(*continued*)

---

[1] The search on the databases was carried out in April 14, 2021.

Table 1. (*continued*)

Year	Authors of the article	Topic of the study
2017	Hong et al. [8]	Connect hearing-impaired elderly with family to improve social life
2017	Ramljak [18]	Medication reminder and monitoring system
2017	Voit et al. [7]	Smart calendar to encourage healthy aging activities
2016	Mainetti et al. [19]	IoT system for health reminders
2016	Kotevski et al. [20]	E-health monitoring and reminder system
2015	Hammer et al. [21]	Lifestyle recommender system
2015	Ribeiro et al. [22]	Health care application

Table 2. Notifications' guidelines for the TV ecosystem

Year	Authors of the article	Topic of the study
2021	Gavrila et al. [5]	HbbTV Smart Home unified experience
2020	Porcu et al. [23]	HbbTV Smart Home system eye gaze analysis
2020	Silva et al. [24]	TV Companion App to Deliver Discount Coupons
2019	Silva et al. [3]	Managing privacy in multiple devices
2018	Anyfantis et al. [25]	TV role in Smart Home environments
2018	Schnauber-Stockmann et al. [26]	Media selection and attention in second-screens
2018	Voit et al. [2]	Multi-device notifications
2018	Yoong et al. [1]	Smart-devices notifications
2017	Guebli and Belkhir [27]	Smart Home with IoT-based TV-box
2016	Abreu et al. [28]	Notifications in second-screens
2016	Weber et al. [11]	Guidelines for notifications on SmartTVs
2015	Almeida et al. [4]	Notifications in second-screens

Results. As the sample was mapped based on two dominant subject matters identified in the articles, for clarity the results are also presented according to those groups, followed by the main insights that supported the design of the use scenarios.

Notifications for Senior Audiences Regarding Remote Care and Health. The provision of useful information and means of communication with family and caregivers, allowing health monitoring and alerts, were the main topics of research in 13 of the 25 analysed studies targeting older adults' audiences (Table 1). This result demonstrates that telecare services are a prolific domain of e-health for the elderly. The assessment of prototypes that integrate the TV with other devices demonstrated the relevance and practicality of sending health reminders, which can be programmed by family, caregivers and health professionals [7, 13–16, 19–22]. In the sample, systems were also evaluated for specific situations, namely the detection of falls aimed at people who live alone, by using sensors and sending notifications to family members through the TV [7]. Other authors [8] present a system that aims to improve the social life of hearing-impaired elderly, by sending notifications to the TV whenever they receive a call, with features like transcribing the conversation and sending images to the screen so they can feel closer to their relatives and friends. Another study tested the integration of a family calendar for sending reminders of events to promote active ageing [7]. A prototype was also evaluated to display Facebook notifications and messages on the TV to connect senior audiences to their families [6], which has advantages in terms of accessibility regarding the size of the screen as well as the visual and textual elements in the interface, as outlined in the study of a system for SmartTVs concerning alerts for medication administration [15].

Notification Guidelines for the TV Ecosystem. The second segment of the sample (Table 2), including 12 studies, is dedicated to relevant aspects for designing notifications aimed at the television ecosystem. The work of [11] presents guidelines for notifications on SmartTVs, with some highlights on how to improve their usability: display only priority information for the user; consider the privacy of each user when the television is shared; present notifications between programs and in a subtle way and; allow easy customization of presentation settings (size, intrusion type and frequency). Privacy was a prominent topic in studies [3] and [25]. In the latter, the evaluated prototype enabled the configuration of how to display notifications on TV in the presence of other people [25]. In the study [3], notifications were addressed through an IoT system using sensors, with proactive reminders sent to different devices (including SmartTV) using several formats (e.g. visual, audio or vibration/touch). Besides health information, this study also tested alerts for controlling home devices (e.g. notification of closing the windows when the weather predicts rain).

Within the scope of content discovery and the synergy between TV and smartphone as a second-screen, the studies [4, 26–28] addressed user preferences for sending personalized notifications to recommend specific content. In the study [24] a companion app was used to provide discount coupons associated with the content being viewed on TV. The studies [5, 23] focused on the use of IoT Hybrid Broadcast Broadband TV (HbbTV) with the integration of other devices based on an IoT system to create an intelligent home environment, including the testing of users' receptiveness to notifications about domestic activities (e.g. warning that the washing cycle was over; showing the video of the entrance door when someone rings the bell, etc.) [23]. In general, participants appreciated notifications, although those accompanied by sounds had lower acceptance. On the other hand, this type of format was the one that most caught the users' attention.

In addition to the mentioned advantages (pros), the negative aspects (cons) regard the excess of notifications and the typology of the format that can become less readable or more disruptive to the tasks at hand. According to [5], some guidelines for formats and notification display should be considered: text messages are less intrusive while audio and video notifications had slightly lower acceptance; the advised position is in the upper right corner of the screen; the ideal average display time is 9 s, as very short intervals hinder the comprehension of the messages. In the study [2], participants complained about the excess of notifications on other devices expressing concern about the proliferation of notifications on the TV. A negative perception of a high number of notifications was also confirmed in the study [1]. Therefore, similarly to other personal devices, it is also necessary in the context of TV to balance the amount of information in each message and the number of notifications to avoid causing anxiety and disturbing the viewing experience. The study [28] also mentions the cognitive disruption that notifications may cause to the TV experience, despite their effectiveness in alerting users to new information and personalized recommendations.

The data considered more relevant from the literature to design the notifications scenarios oriented to the TV ecosystem were: useful location-based information (e.g. weather, traffic, news, etc.); info related to the content being viewed and the users' preferences; social communications; calendar appointments and local events; as well as recommendation of services and apps; recommendation of health and well-being behaviours and medication alerts. In terms of formats, textual and sound notifications were considered for the TV remote control interactions and the tablet and smartphone as companion second-screens. Voice interaction was also considered relevant to be presented to the participants of the focus group since VUIs have proven to be the direction of the industry [29].

3.2 Focus Group

Protocol and Sample Characterization. With the goal of developing a prototype for a field trial in collaboration with a Portuguese Pay-TV provider, the next step after gathering information from the literature review was to systematize six thematic domains to design use scenarios (Table 3) which were presented in one focus group with potential users[2].

Table 3. Use scenarios presented in the focus group

Scenario	Thematic domain	Objective
1	CONTENT (TV and over-the-top)	To recommend content based on users habits and provide access to content-related features;
2	SOCIAL (telecommunications and social media)	To inform that the user has received a message with the aim of promoting socialization;
3	SERVICES (apps, online shopping and coupons)	To inform the schedule of a TV live content and suggest a food delivery service;

(*continued*)

---

[2] The focus group was carried out in January 17, 2022.

Table 3. (*continued*)

Scenario	Thematic domain	Objective
4	HEALTH (monitoring and well-being recommendations)	To alert about health monitoring information and encourage socialization and well-being behaviors, namely outdoors;
5	CALENDAR (personal, shared and local appointments and events)	To alert about the date of a school assignment and recommend YouTube content, as well as a local event related to the subject of the test;
6	INFO (useful information)	To provide information about the local weather and give practical and security advice

The focus group aimed to gather information about the relevance of those scenarios and to identify other use cases regarding the TV ecosystem at home. Thus, by adopting a TV-first approach, attention was given to diversified household dynamics among participants and recruiting a manageable group of participants so the interventions could be lengthier and less contaminated [30]. With this in mind, participants living with roommates, children, elderly and couples were included so they could bring different viewing experiences.

The six scenarios associated to each thematic domain were presented sequentially during a 60 min session in a setup with a living room configuration (see Fig. 1). The session was recorded with the consent of the participants for content analysis. Before the beginning of the session, each participant responded to a brief characterization questionnaire about audiovisual content consumption and use of devices and features (e.g. intelligent assistants; smart devices; voice commands; smart home devices; media players connected to the TV; health monitoring devices; smartwatches, etc.). After each video with the scenarios, participants manifested their opinion and gave suggestions of other possible uses. During the final part of the session were also discussed issues about privacy, the number of notifications on multiple devices, the use of voice commands and which specific situations, formats and devices they would find more relevant to receive notifications. The participants were encouraged to express themselves freely during the sessions and present suggestions and opinions also about their relatives' uses (e.g., parents, offspring, grandparents, mates, etc.).

The sample consisted of six participants, four female and two male, aged between 17 and 47 years, two with a PhD, three with a master's degree and one with basic education attending secondary education. Each element of the sample represented different types of households so the dynamics with the shared TV at home would be reflected in their opinions and suggestions. Thus, three participants had a household with children and adults, another participant shared a house with family members and adult friends, one of whom was over 65 years old, another participant lived with his girlfriend, and the youngest participant who, despite living with both parents and siblings, indicated that

Fig. 1. Living room setup (left) and focus group session (right).

watched TV alone. Only one of the participants did not subscribe to a Pay-TV provider, but used the Chromecast device to watch other content on TV in addition to the nine channels of the Digital TV service in Portugal. All participants subscribed to Netflix (but one of the participants used only one profile for the whole family, including children) and, themselves or someone in their household (e.g. children), watched YouTube videos through SmartTV or connecting the tablet or mobile phone to the TV set. One of the participants used a game console connected to the TV, and two of the participants use Smart Home devices (one uses Alexa and the other uses Google Home). Five out of six participants watched TV at least once a day. Only the youngest participant mentioned less regularity, watching TV only a few times a week. In terms of features and devices, half of the sample never used Smart Home devices. Regarding the use of smart assistants on mobile devices, two participants always use them, three use them on certain apps and devices and only one participant never used it at all.

Results. To facilitate the presentation of the results, a synthesis of the feedback about each scenario is presented individually followed by the discussion in the next section. All the animations suggested a TV-first approach being the notification announced by a sound alert and delivered by a voice message during a TV commercial, to indicate that there would not be an intrusion of a content being viewed. Nevertheless, the participants were informed that this was merely an example and the notifications could be received in other devices and in other media formats according to their preferences, because that was exactly the kind of feedback we intended to collect during the session. The textual messages in the figures bellow are illustrative of the notification content and were also shown as a static frame during the discussion after the end of each video animation to remind the participants of the voice notification.

Scenario 1 - CONTENT. In this scenario (see Fig. 2) a couple is watching TV and a notification indicates that a series of the same genre the user usually watches will premiere within three days on a specific channel. Then, another notification asks if the user wants to program the recording of the season, which is one of the features of the TV set-top box.

One of the participants suggested that the information could be more precise, by displaying the day of the week and the schedule of the show for the user to decide whether to record or watch live. Furthermore, participants suggested that the notification made more sense for a collective profile of the couple due to being presented on a shared

Fig. 2. Excerpt from animation of use scenario 1 presented in the focus group.

TV, in addition to having the advantage of not contaminating the recommendations of the individual profile. Another suggestion, when using individual profiles of users that watch the same series, was the possibility of having one functionality that could inform the user if the other profile has already seen a specific episode to wait or notify him to watch together.

Participants considered appealing to encourage the discovery of content related to their interests and the discovery of new channels, because their Pay-TV services often include a wide range of channels but they frequently end up using always the same. On the other hand, some participants mentioned that the recommendations by interests are restrictive because there is much content they don't know if they like and never saw anything similar, but because of the way the recommender systems work may never be recommended to them. In this case, one participant manifested more interest and curiosity in social recommendations, even though it is not the type of content she usually watches, because she values the taste of her friends and colleagues. In addition, this type of social recommendation would also encourage conversation and possibly collective viewing sessions, bringing people together and promoting conviviality and socialization.

Scenario 2 - SOCIAL. In this scenario (see Fig. 3), a girl is watching TV alone, because when designing the scenario some reservations have already been anticipated regarding the display of social messages in a shared screen. Nevertheless, throughout the session we reminded the participants that they should express their preferences about how and on which devices they would like to receive and reply to notifications. The notification of the SOCIAL scenario refers to a message from a group chat, regarding a series that they are following. The subsequent notification asks if the user wants to see the message. In this case, the objective was to open the discussion about the devices in which the participants preferred to continue the interactions potentially driven by the notification.

Participants were unanimous in their preference for receiving social messages on personal devices, in particular the mobile phone. Notifications on the TV would only be well received if that device is for personal use or is located in a private space such as an office or bedroom. However, children who are used to connecting devices to the TV, such as tablets and game consoles, would have fewer problems receiving notifications in a shared space or device. In the case of the elderly it would be advantageous to receive messages on the TV given the screen size being larger. Participants mentioned examples of their parents and grandparents who have difficulties not only switching

Fig. 3. Excerpt from animation of use scenario 2 presented in the focus group.

between devices but specifically typing text messages. In this case, voice messages and video calls were suggested as useful alternatives, although it was warned that they would probably need help.

Scenario 3 - SERVICES. In this scenario (see Fig. 4) several people are watching TV and the notification message suggests a collective profile ('PartyPeople') that indicates a shared household dynamic, possibly with student housemates. The notification informs that a live football match will start shortly. The second notification asks if they want to order food, indicating a georeferenced service.

Fig. 4. Excerpt from animation of use scenario 3 presented in the focus group.

Participants found this contextual suggestion close to mealtime very useful. They even mentioned the advantage of browsing the app on the TV to choose the food together. Nonetheless, they preferred to finish the transaction more privately through the mobile phone. They also mentioned the request for a transportation service (e.g. Uber) through the same system in the case of late dinners when there is no longer public transport or when some friends have had too much to drink or are tired and prefer not to drive. An example mentioned as an undesirable suggestion of services and products was recommending a book that exists from a movie they are watching. In this sense, the participants were unanimous about the value of a configuration feature for which apps and services they wanted to receive notifications.

Scenario 4 - HEALTH. This scenario (see Fig. 5) suggests the articulation between the TV and the smartwatch to monitor the heartbeat. As in the SOCIAL scenario, the animation presents a person watching TV alone because some reservations were also anticipated regarding HEALTH notifications in a shared device. The scenario comprises the display of a sequence of three notifications: the first informs that the heart rate is a little high; the second gives a suggestion, to invite friends for a walk and; the third notification suggests a podcast.

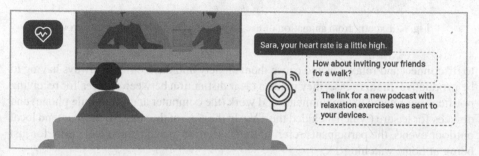

Fig. 5. Excerpt from animation of use scenario 4 presented in the focus group.

The participants considered this scenario the most invasive, mainly because the information is very personal and causes stress, even when received on the mobile phone, despite that being the preferred device for receiving this type of information. None of the participant would like to receive these notifications on the TV, even if they lived alone, because it would disturb the state of relaxation and immersion, which is usual when watching TV. However, in the context of HEALTH, some participants mentioned that they use screen time managing systems with their younger children for scheduling breaks. Thus, a similar approach was suggested towards the elderly for recommending pauses for stretching exercises when facing sedentary lifestyles and long periods of inactivity in front of the TV, and even to remind of regular fluid intake. Another recurrent aspect mentioned for this audience are the notifications to remind of regular medication intake. In short, this scenario was totally discarded by the participants for their own use, but was considered very useful for senior audiences depending on the type of information and how is communicated to avoid alarming them.

Regarding the other displayed notifications, namely inviting friends for a walk and suggesting a podcast, the participants did not express much feedback, mentioning that they could be interesting although they needed to understand better how the system would actually work to perform those tasks.

Scenario 5 - CALENDAR. This scenario (see Fig. 6) presents a family watching TV and the notification addresses one of the children to alert about the approaching date of a school test. A second notification informs about a local event related to the subject matter of the test. And the following notification asks if he wants to add suggestions of YouTube channels related to the topic to his list of favourites.

All the participants mentioned that CALENDAR notifications on the TV – a device they mostly use at night after school and after work as a break moment when they want

Fig. 6. Excerpt from animation of use scenario 5 presented in the focus group.

to disconnect and relax – would cause them anxiety and the feeling of always having to be productive. In this sense, they made a clear distinction between devices for receiving notifications related to appointments and work (the computer and the mobile phone) and devices for leisure (which included the TV). In the case of the suggestions to attend local outdoor events, the participants referred that it seemed to make them feel guilty for just being at home watching TV.

In the specific case of the recommendation of YouTube content related to the subject of a school test, it was mentioned that it could cause misinformation given the amount of material that is available online and the specifics of the test.

However, the CALENDAR thematic domain was considered useful for the elderly that frequently forget tasks and appointments. Hence, the participants suggested some examples of notifications, like reminders of medical consultations, bill payments and municipal services deadlines and even maintenance services such as car inspection.

Scenario 6 - INFO. This scenario (see Fig. 7) suggests that the user is getting ready to leave and the notification informs him of the forecast of heavy rain for his location. A subsequent notification advises him to drive with caution and carry an umbrella.

Fig. 7. Excerpt from animation of use scenario 6 presented in the focus group.

This scenario was the one that had the most positive reaction from the participants, given the practical use it would have in their daily lives. As it is not a notification with personal information, the reception in the shared TV was well-received, namely when the family gathers in the morning, before leaving for work and school, and at night for those who prefer to prepare clothes and accessories according to the forecast for the next day.

One participant mentioned that he schedules a morning routine on his Alexa device to receive voice notifications in the morning with all his appointments for the day, suggesting that this new system could aggregate several types of information in the daily routine. This participant showed interest in receiving notifications on the TV in audio format so that he could listen to them while getting ready to go out. In addition to the weather forecast, the participants suggested other types of information for these morning and end-of-day notification routines, namely: the on-duty pharmacies; transport timetables; warnings about interruptions or strikes in transport, schools and public services; changes in fuel prices; changes in the opening hours of establishments and services due to holidays, etc.

4 Discussion of the Results

The insights from the literature, regarding target audiences, types of information, application contexts, and guidelines for the notifications, confirmed its potential towards the TV ecosystem, by highlighting some possible use scenarios, namely: sending personalized recommendations and promoting interactions about the content being viewed; for targeted advertising; for location-based information and events; for promoting social communication based on content or events; for calendar alerts and; for health alerts and monitoring.

After the systematization of the insights obtained in the literature review, the six use scenarios were designed with an emphasis on the use of the TV at home and were presented in one focus group to discuss their relevance and collect suggestions. The qualitative analysis of the focus group data provided additional significant inputs for the prototyping phase, namely about the relevance given to the personalization of formats, preferred input/output devices and the intrusion moments for the reception of notifications. It also highlighted the differences between user profiles that seem to be related to age groups, viewing habits, use of connected devices and gamming behaviours, as well as the household routines.

Overall, the most-well received scenarios by the participants were: 1) INFO, comprising notifications integrated in a morning routine with the information for the day and, in the evening with the information for the next day); 2) CONTENT, namely the discovery of unexplored TV channels and, social suggestions from friends regarding what they are currently watching and what they enjoyed watching; 3) SERVICES, although only allowing specific apps selected by the user.

The CALENDAR, HEALTH and SOCIAL scenarios were the less appealing and usable for the participants. Being the HEALTH and SOCIAL scenarios considered very intrusive and disruptive, raising privacy issues due to the fact that the shared TV presented on the videos in the living room suggested that was the main device for the notifications (since we were probing a TV-first approach although not exclusive). All the participants preferred to receive the notifications of those scenarios on their smartphones. However, in the SOCIAL scenario, it was mentioned that there would be no restraint by the elderly (parents and grandparents) to communicate with family members and by their younger children who watch online videos and forums connected to the TV. Another participant, who is a gamer, mentioned he would not bother either. In the case of the HEALTH scenario, it was also considered useful for seniors to remember regular medication intake and the CALENDAR notification to remember medical appointments and bill payments.

In the HEALTH and CALENDAR scenarios, respectively the example of mentioning the accelerated heartbeat and remembering a school exam, the participants referred that caused stress and anxiety when being presented on TV that should be a moment of relaxation. Also, the suggestion to do physical activities and attend to local events outdoors seemed discouraging of that moment when they just want to watch TV and stay at home. Hence, the group of participants made a clear distinction between devices associated with work (computer and mobile phone) and associated with leisure (TV).

However, some scenarios that were discarded by this group aged 17–47 were mentioned as advantageous for their older relatives, namely HEALTH scenarios (because they frequently forget daily tasks) and SOCIAL (because they do not have such a close relationship with the mobile phone and the screen is smaller). The INFO and CALENDAR scenarios were also considered useful for elderly to remember appointments and outdoor activities, since some of them are already retired and there is no longer that distinction between work and leisure time. In addition, they usually spend more time at home with the TV that becomes a companion instead of a device to watch a specific content. Therefore, in view of these hypotheses/assumptions put forward by the participants about their older family members, another focus group was held with seniors, to validate the interest in health monitoring scenarios and social scenarios, as well as useful information and local events, to promote sociability and active aging.

Regarding the formats for the notifications, the participants were not consensual. Some preferred more discrete visual alerts like small icons. Others preferred sound notifications, mentioning that they would otherwise pass unnoticed, especially for the elderly like their grandparents that are more distracted by all the visual elements on the screen.

In what concerns the devices, because this was a group with higher academic education (only a participant was a seventeen-year-old student attending secondary school) they mentioned the computer and the mobile phone as work-related devices in which they preferred to receive SOCIAL and HEALTH notification privately. But they stated that their parents and grandparents would prefer to receive those notifications in the bigger TV screen, that is often connected all the time at home and because most of the time those relatives do not carry or cannot easily find their mobile phone. On the other hand, TV was mentioned as the preferred device to relax, watching movies, series, and online videos, as well as for receiving CONTENT notifications for collective profiles and INFO notifications directed to all the family, such as the weather, fuel rates, transportation strikes, local news, etc. The CALENDAR notifications, such as appointments, were also mentioned to be relevant in morning or evening alerts.

When discussing the reply to SOCIAL notifications, the participants prefer texting on the mobile phone, whereas older people (their parents or grandparents) would prefer voice messages and, if possible, video calls on the TV, despite some literacy difficulties that probably would require help. So, we can affirm that personalization of what the user wants to receive – what, how and when – is the key to notifications, including in the TV ecosystem that has a great potential dealing with different household dynamics, which generate many use scenarios that can be explored. Therefore, some of the next steps are testing prototypes with different age groups to grasp a personalization solution that can tackle the needs of different user profiles.

5 Conclusions and Future Work

Based on the analysed studies from the literature review, notifications were confirmed as a relevant mechanism with potential towards the TV ecosystem for sending personalized content and promoting interactions about the content being viewed. This strategy is also used with marketing purposes, such as targeted advertising with benefits for the user. In some of the reviewed studies, notifications were tested for providing location-based information and useful reminders about daily activities, with particular emphasis on health alerts and medication monitoring for the elderly. The promotion of communication and connecting individuals was addressed in fewer studies, being a topic that needed further exploration. From these insights, six thematic domains focused on a TV-first approach were systematized: CONTENT; SOCIAL, SERVICES; HEALTH; CALENDAR; INFO. For each domain a use scenario was designed having in consideration group dynamics from different households (e.g. families with children, couples, younger housemates, senior couples and people living alone). The scenarios were presented in one focus group to assess their relevance, collect suggestions of other scenarios, and probe the potential of notifications for the TV ecosystem. The focus group session was very prolific because of the feedback provided by the participants about their household routines, which are crucial to the scenarios of notifications to be displayed specially at home in the shared TV screen.

The overall results affirmed the personalization of what the user wants to receive, when and on which device as key to notifications also in the TV ecosystem. Based on the feedback of the participants, who evoked their household routines in the focus group discussion, the next step is to carry out laboratory tests with a prototype to validate interface options, presentation formats, intrusion moments, dimensions and other visual, textual and audio elements before moving on to field trials.

Because of the opinions put forward by the participants about their older family members, a second focus group with elderly people has already been carried out and the preliminary analysis of the results partially corroborates some of the anticipated assumptions. Meanwhile, an intermediate laboratory test phase is being prepared to fine-tune the interface of notifications on the TV. In a third step, field trials will be carried out to evaluate the User Experience (UX) over time. For each user, a set of personalized notifications will be identified through previous questionnaires and will be scheduled using a management platform developed within this research, and delivered though the IPTV partners' infrastructure.

Hence, the data gathered though the literature review and the focus groups supported the preparation of the UX testing of a notifications' prototype in collaboration with a Portuguese Pay-TV provider, to possibly introduce some features in their service. In short, from this study we can anticipate that the television ecosystem has a promising potential in synergy with connected devices (such as the mobile phone, tablet and smart-watch) and within the dynamics of individual and group viewing associated to different households.

Acknowledgments. Altice Labs@UA, a research group resulting from the partnership between Altice Portugal and the University of Aveiro, funded this research.

References

1. Yoong, S., López, G., Guerrero, L.A.: Smart device-based notifications: a survey on user's satisfaction of traditional notification mechanisms. In: Ho, A. (ed.) Advances in Communication of Design. AHFE 2017. Advances in Intelligent Systems and Computing, vol. 609. Springer, Cham. https://doi.org/10.1007/978-3-319-60477-0_12

2. Voit, A., Weber, D., Henze, N.: Qualitative investigation of multi-device notifications. In: UbiComp/ISWC 2018, pp. 1263–1270 (2018). https://doi.org/10.1145/3267305.3274117

3. Silva, L.A., Leithardt, V.R.Q., Rolim, C.O., González, G.V., Geyer, C.F.R., Silva, J.S.: Priser: managing notification in multiple devices with data privacy support. Sensors (Switzerland) **19**(14), 1–18 (2019). https://doi.org/10.3390/s19143098

4. Almeida, P., Abreu, J., Silva, T., Duro, L., Aresta, M., Oliveira, R.: Notification mechanisms in second-screen scenarios towards a balanced user experience. In: Proceedings of the 2015 7th International Conference on Intelligent Technologies for Interactive Entertainment, INTETAIN (2015). https://doi.org/10.4108/icst.intetain.2015.259548

5. Gavrila, C., Popescu, V., Fadda, M., Anedda, M., Murroni, M.: On the suitability of HbbTV for unified smart home experience. IEEE Trans. Broadcast. **67**(1), 253–262 (2021). https://doi.org/10.1109/TBC.2020.2977539

6. Coelho, J., Rito, F., Duarte, C.: "You, me & TV"—fighting social isolation of older adults with Facebook, TV and multimodality. Int. J. Hum. Comput. Stud. **98**, 38–50 (2017). https://doi.org/10.1016/j.ijhcs.2016.09.015

7. Voit, A., Weber, D., Stowell, E., Henze, N.: Caloo: an ambient pervasive smart calendar to support aging in place. In: ACM International Conference Proceeding Series, pp. 25–30 (2017). https://doi.org/10.1145/3152832.3152847

8. Hong, H.T., Su, T.Y., Lee, P.H., Hsieh, P.C., Chiu, M.J.: VisualLink: strengthening the connection between hearing-impaired elderly and their family (2017). https://doi.org/10.1145/3027063.3049269

9. Mehrotra, A., Pejovic, V., Vermeulen, J., Hendley, R., Musolesi, M.: My phone and me: understanding people's receptivity to mobile notification. In: Proceedings of CHI 2016, pp. 1021–1032 (2016). http://dl.acm.org/citation.cfm?doid=2858036.2858566

10. Wheatley, D., Ferrer-Conill, R.: The temporal nature of mobile push notification alerts: a study of European news outlets' dissemination patterns. Digit. J. **9**(6), 694–714 (2021). https://doi.org/10.1080/21670811.2020.1799425

11. Weber, D., Mayer, S., Voit, A., Fierro, R.V., Henze, N.: Design guidelines for notifications on smart TVs. In: TVX 2016 - Proceedings of the ACM International Conference on Interactive Experiences for TV and Online Video, pp. 13–24 (2016). https://doi.org/10.1145/2932206.2932212

12. Kita, T., Nagaoka, C., Hiraoka, N., Suzuki, K., Dougiamas, M.: A discussion on effective implementation and prototyping of voice user interfaces for learning activities on moodle. In: CSEDU 2018 - Proceedings of the 10th International Conference on Computer Supported Education (2018). https://doi.org/10.5220/0006782603980404

13. MacIs, S., et al.: Design and usability assessment of a multi-device SOA-based telecare framework for the elderly. IEEE J. Biomed. Health Inform. **24**(1), 268–279 (2020). https://doi.org/10.1109/JBHI.2019.2894552
14. Corcella, L., Manca, M., Nordvik, J.E., Paternò, F., Sanders, A.-M., Santoro, C.: Enabling personalisation of remote elderly assistance. Multimed. Tools Appl. **78**(15), 21557–21583 (2019). https://doi.org/10.1007/s11042-019-7449-z
15. Santana-Mancilla, P.C., Anido-Rifón, L.E.: iTVCare: a home care system for the elderly through interactive television. Avances En Interacción Humano-Computadora **3**(1), 92 (2018). https://doi.org/10.47756/aihc.y3i1.56
16. Silva, T., Caravau, H., Carvalho, D.: Comparative usability study of an iTV interface for seniors. In: ACM International Conference Proceeding Series, pp. 310–316 (2018). https://doi.org/10.1145/3218585.3218675
17. Watanapa, B., Patsadu, O., Dajpratham, P., Nukoolkit, C.: Post-fall intelligence supporting fall severity diagnosis using kinect sensor. Appl. Comput. Intell. Soft Comput. **2018**(3), 1–15 (2018). https://doi.org/10.1155/2018/5434897
18. Ramljak, M.: Smart home medication reminder system. In: 2017 25th International Conference on Software, Telecommunications and Computer Networks, SoftCOM 2017 (2017). https://doi.org/10.23919/SOFTCOM.2017.8115585
19. Mainetti, L., Patrono, L., Secco, A., Sergi, I.: An IoT-aware AAL system for elderly people, pp. 1–6 (2016). https://doi.org/10.1109/SpliTech.2016.7555929
20. Kotevski, A., Koceska, N., Koceski, S.: E-health monitoring system (2016). https://doi.org/10.20544/AIIT2016.3
21. Hammer, S., et al.: Design of a lifestyle recommender system for the elderly, pp. 1–8 (2015). https://doi.org/10.1145/2769493.2769559
22. Ribeiro, V.S., Martins, A.I., Queirós, A., Silva, A.G., Rocha, N.P.: Usability evaluation of a health care application based on IPTV. Procedia Comput. Sci. **64**, 635–642 (2015). https://doi.org/10.1016/j.procs.2015.08.577
23. Porcu, S., Floris, A., Anedda, M., Popescu, V., Fadda, M., Atzori, L.: Quality of experience eye gaze analysis on HbbTV smart home notification system (2020). https://doi.org/10.1109/BMSB49480.2020.9379794
24. Silva, T., Almeida, P., Cardoso, B., Oliveira, R., Cunha, A., Ribeiro, C.: Smartly: a TV companion app to deliver discount coupons. In: Abásolo, M.J., Kulesza, R., Pina Amargós, J.D. (eds.) jAUTI 2019. CCIS, vol. 1202, pp. 53–66. Springer, Cham (2020). https://doi.org/10.1007/978-3-030-56574-9_4
25. Anyfantis, N., et al.: AmITV: enhancing the role of TV in ambient intelligence environments (2018). https://doi.org/10.1145/3197768.3201548
26. Schnauber-Stockmann, A., Meier, A., Reinecke, L.: Procrastination out of habit? The role of impulsive versus reflective media selection in procrastinatory media use. Media Psychol. **21**(4), 640–668 (2018). https://doi.org/10.1080/15213269.2018.1476156
27. Guebli, W., Belkhir, A.: TV home-box based IoT for smart home. In: ACM International Conference Proceeding Series (2017). https://doi.org/10.1145/3175628.3175634
28. Abreu, J., Almeida, P., Silva, T., Aresta, M.: Notifications efficiency, impact, and interference in second-screen scenarios. Int. J. Hum.-Comput. Interact. **32**(12), 901–911 (2016). https://doi.org/10.1080/10447318.2016.1210870
29. Fernandes, S., Abreu, J., Almeida, P., Santos, R.: A review of voice user interfaces for interactive TV. In: Abásolo, M.J., Silva, T., González, N.D. (eds.) jAUTI 2018. CCIS, vol. 1004, pp. 115–128. Springer, Cham (2019). https://doi.org/10.1007/978-3-030-23862-9_9
30. Kruger, R.A., Casey, M.A.: Focus Groups. A Practical Guide for Applied Research. Sage, USA (2015)

Connect Elderly to Other Generations Through iTV: Evaluating Notifications' Potential

Juliana Camargo(✉) ⓘ, Telmo Silva ⓘ, and Jorge Abreu ⓘ

DigiMedia, Department of Communication and Arts, University of Aveiro, Aveiro, Portugal
{julianacamargo,tsilva,jfa}@ua.pt

Abstract. Television is among the preferred technological devices of the elderly due to their familiarity with its simple interface and because it acts as a sort of companion, being this especially relevant for those living alone. This phenomenon was particularly observed during the social isolation resulting from the Covid-19 pandemic. In the most critical period of the health crisis, the consumption of television content among older people and the adoption of other digital solutions aimed at entertainment or social interaction increased significantly. At the same time, technological advances in the television ecosystem have made it possible to include resources capable of making the gadget increasingly interactive and friendly. An example is the use of notifications, a mechanism that consists in displaying messages on the device's screen, engaging users to a specific topic. TV notifications can act as an information-focused tool with the potential to promote the connection of seniors with their family or friends. In the aforementioned context, the objective of this paper is to identify how TV notifications can contribute to reduce the rates of social isolation among the elderly, offering new forms of interaction with society. For, initially, a literature review was carried out to allow contextualizing the problem. Studies conducted in this field were evaluated to identify whether the television ecosystem would be able to enhance human relationship. These studies supported the construction of a questionnaire focused on identifying the habits of the elderly in relation to the adoption of technological devices, the consumption of television content and the acceptance of notifications in this context. Therefore, this study provides evidence that notifications can connect generations, being an important mechanism to reduce the rates of loneliness among older individuals.

Keywords: Elderly · Seniors · notifications · Social isolation · TV · iTV

1 Introduction

Television is a device often used by the elderly, especially when they feel alone [1]. Social isolation is recurrent among these individuals being the main reasons that keep them from social life are physical disabilities and low education [2]. This situation intensified during the Covid-19 disease pandemic, which significantly increased the consumption of television content among older people, as well as the adoption of other technological resources aimed at entertainment and social interaction [3]. Since family members were further away due to the health crisis, videoconferences and social networks helped to

M. J. Abásolo and G. F. Olmedo Cifuentes (Eds.): jAUTI 2021, CCIS 1597, pp. 20–35, 2022.
https://doi.org/10.1007/978-3-031-22210-8_2

reduce social isolation [3]. However, while they help, digital resources can represent a barrier, mainly because skepticism about using new technological resources tends to be higher among the elderly [4].

In contrast, advances in Artificial Intelligence (AI) and Big Data have allowed devices to anticipate users' needs, rather than just reacting to them [5, 6]. One example is notifications, a mechanism that directly impacts the public and contributes to stimulate the use of digital resources [30, 31].

Based on this perspective, the objective is to identify if such messages (used in the television ecosystem) can increase the elderly contact with other people, thus reducing social isolation rates. For that, this article was divided into four parts. The first brings data on the rates of isolation among the elderly. Next, it is based on the detailing of the methodology used in the selection of articles and for the characterization of the identified sample. Such studies served as a basis for structuring a questionnaire about preferences in relation to TV and the use of technologies that help to keep in touch with other people. This process is detailed in Sect. 3, which also contains the characterization of the sample of 20 senior citizens who were interviewed for the present study.

Section 4 presents the main results, organized into two parts: literature review and interviews. Finally, there are the final considerations, which pointed the benefits of the study to the television ecosystem and the senior audience. Still in this section there is also a brief explanation of future work in this area.

2 Technology to Promote Interactions

During the COVID-19 pandemic, which started in March 2020, the need for social isolation forced people to stay in their homes and use digital platforms to minimize the effects of confinement [7]. In the case of the elderly, this imposition was even more significant because of the higher risks involved– the deaths of individuals over 65 years of age correspond to 80% in the United States and 95% in Europe [8]. This scenario enhanced the levels of loneliness of the senior public, who historically suffered from problems related to lack of contact [2].

In Portugal, it is estimated that 42,434 elderly people are isolated, in a situation of vulnerability due to their physical and psychological conditions [9]. The pandemic, in turn, contributed to amplify the problem, evidencing the need to provide means for this public to maintain healthy relationships and actively participate in communities.

One way to minimize social isolation rates is using mobile devices and resources such as videoconferencing and gaming, for example [10]. However, incorporating them into everyday life can still represent a barrier for older people due to several factors – and one of the main factors is its difficulty of use [2]. Not always the senior possesses sufficient skills or familiarity with technological resources [3]. And this is the result of several factors, such as skepticism about innovative technologies and rapid renouncement when facing difficulties related to usage [4]. Since there is a barrier, mechanisms that require less cognitive effort, such as notifications, are a way to facilitate the usage of technological resources [11]. By being proactively sent to seniors, these messages enable access to information and to other people, stimulating the connection between individuals [12]. In addition, notifications facilitate access to newly available information, making the user's attention turn to the content in question [13]. It is an element considered important in the communication ecosystem because it directly impacts the public without intermediaries, inducing the user to view specific information and be received from different devices, such as the TV set [14]. Such messages can have different formats (visual, auditory or vibration/touch alerts), increasing accessibility [15]. In addition, especially in the case of the elderly, notifications usually send reminders of important activities, for instance medication schedules or appointments on the agenda (Fig. 1). Health-monitoring applications can also send frequent bulletins to the family or caregivers [24], reaffirming the multiplicity of functions and possibilities of this type of mechanism.

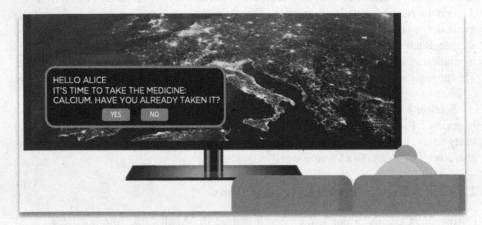

Fig. 1. Example of how notifications can be displayed on TV to send health alerts.

3   Methodology

3.1   Literature Review Protocol and Sample Characterization

A survey was carried out to identify the potential of notifications to reduce the rates of social isolation among seniors. Therefore, the methodology of a systematic review of the PRISMA model was chosen [16] to carry out the work. A review protocol was defined based on a research protocol with three groups of keywords on the SCOPUS and Web of Science platforms. The first survey was conducted at SCOPUS, between July 12 and 15, 2021, with "elderly AND notification AND social AND isolation AND television OR TV". 18 results were found, and after reading all abstracts, it was identified that only 3 were pertinent. Studies that do not address the use of notifications directly on the television screen were excluded. Then, a second search with the following terms "notification AND television OR tv OR iTV AND elderly" had 76 results. All abstracts were re-evaluated and only three were considered relevant.

Both searches were also performed on the Web of Science platform, and the results considered relevant were repeated. To verify that the keywords chosen were the most appropriate, we chose to search the Web of Science more widely with the words "elderly

AND TV OR television". A total of 111 results were found, which had their abstracts evaluated. Only 9 of them were related to the use of notifications on TV. In total, therefore, 15 studies were evaluated. All the texts in the sample are in English and present the notifications displayed on television as possible mechanisms to make relevant information more easily reach users.

In the SCOPUS sample, 67% (4) studies are about social contacts, 17% (1) about health and 17% (1) refer to the format of display on the screen. In the Web of Science sample, 22% (2) refer to the format/design, 44% (4) contribute to promoting health, 22% (2) integrate Smart Home circuits and 11% (1) are about education.

3.2 Interviews Protocol and Sample Characterization

As mentioned, the scientific mapping performed in the initial phase of this study served as the basis for the creation of a questionnaire that was later applied to a group of 20 elderly. The interviews had three specific objectives: i) to characterize the public; ii) identify the relationship of the elderly with technological resources and the consumption of television content; and iii) understand the perception of this public concerning the usage of notifications in the television ecosystem.

In total, there were 30 fixed questions, divided into three sections, created according to the above-mentioned objectives. Additional questions were made during the conversations, as participants said something related to their experiences using electronic devices.

Each interview lasted, on average, 40 min and were conducted from December 2021 to March 2022. In total, 20 elderly people ages between 60 and 95 years participated, 14 Portuguese and six Brazilians (the last six interviews were made by telephone, since the interviewees live in Brazil). Some examples of the questions that were asked with the participants:

- Do you think television is a companion?
- How many hours a day do you watch TV?
- What would you think if messages sent by your family members were displayed on the television screen?
- Do you believe that this kind of message would hinder or add value to your experience of consuming television content?

The average age of the participants was 76.9 years. Regarding gender, 70% (14) are women and 30% (6) men. Of the total number of interviewees, 45% (9) live alone and 55% (11) live with their partner or with their children. When asked about possible physical limitations, 10% (2) said they have hearing loss, although they still listen, and another 10% (2) pointed out that they have difficulty seeing very small letters on television or other electronic devices.

Regarding the use of technological devices to communicate, only 15% (3) stated that they do not have a cell phone and that they communicate with their relatives or caregivers essentially by landline phone. These participants are in the group of respondents over 85 years of age (two people are 87 and one 88 years old). The others stated that they use their cell phones daily. The main activities carried out by senior citizens are described in Fig. 2.

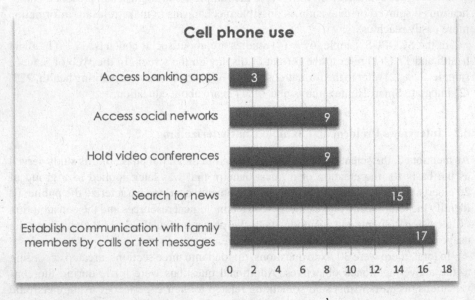

Fig. 2. Reasons why the elderly use the mobile phone (separated by volume of mentions).

Among the participants who have a mobile phone, only 10% (2) stated that the device is not a smartphone. That is, it is a device that only makes calls and sends text messages. "Although I don't have this more advanced phone, I really like making video calls to my grandchildren who live in another country. My daughter comes here every weekend to make the calls. Seeing them is something else, it helps kill the longing and brings us closer. I would adopt knowing how to use this type of resource, but I have difficulties", commented one of the participants, 87 years old.

When asked about the use of notifications on the mobile phone, only two of the 17 individuals who own the device stated that they did not know the meaning of the word "notification". After a brief explanation, they understood its definition and stated that they receive this type of warning daily.

Among the other participants who said they had a mobile phone, all pointed out that they receive daily notifications, especially from banking apps, social media and messaging applications. None of the participants were bothered by this type of functionality. Overall, they said it's "a positive thing and helps inform them about news and updates to the device."

In addition to the mobile phone, 45% (9) of respondents said they have other electronic devices, such as tablets and notebooks, but use them less frequently compared to the phone. According to the interviewees, the main activities performed on these electronic devices are "watching series", "play electronic games" and "accessing websites belonging to local governments". "I prefer to watch movies and series on the tablet because the screen is bigger," said a 77-year-old participant.

Only one participant (90 years old) stated that she has a virtual assistant (Alexa, Amazon) and uses it daily, especially to schedule reminders related to everyday tasks. Finally, two participants (both 64 years old) said they have smartwatches to control health-related aspects and can access messages received on their mobile phones more easily.

All participants were also asked if they have difficulties in the use of technological devices. Only 10% (2) stated that they do not have any type of problem or impediment – these participants are 60 and 77 years old. The other 90% (18) said they have difficulties to use them on a day-to-day life, and 88.8% (16) turn to close relatives to ask questions and 11.2% seek information in tutorials available on the Internet. "My generation has a hard time dealing with technology. I try to learn to the fullest, but there are aspects where I need explanations from the younger ones. Unfortunately, I think there is a barrier to teaching older people, because young people do not always have patience or didactics," commented a 63-year-old participant.

4 Results and Discussion

4.1 Literature Review

The studies [17, 18] and [19] focused on reducing social isolation and have identified that notifications are important mechanisms to attract the attention of the elderly to messages sent by their families or friends. The feature was used to disclose reminders of family commitments [17], send alerts for calls on mobile phones [18] and encourage participation in gamification dynamics [19]. In this last study, the interactions took place by voice, and the intelligent assistant was considered by the elderly a sensitive, sociable and friendly company, able to contribute by itself to reduce the rates of loneliness. Also in this context, [1] focused on creating a prototype of Facebook adapted for television. Seniors positively evaluated the feature in terms of usability and the potential to increase online and offline interactions.

Regarding studies focused on health promotion, the notifications were used in [20–22] to remind seniors about medication schedules, medical care or information related to their well-being. In these cases, in addition to facilitating access to important data, the messages connected the elderly to external issues, which also contributes to the reduction of social isolation. This conclusion was also present in [23], the only article related to education. By analyzing the behavior of older people in the face of messages coming from e-learning applications, television is detected as an important device to promote access to learning. In [24], the authors chose the opposite way: notify the families via television and other devices if the elderly suffered a fall. The multitude of devices helped reduce the waiting time for help.

Of the total articles, three were about the design and messages format. In [25], the use of icons related to messages content facilitated understanding. In [26], it was detected that the use of a virtual assistant, which combines textual and audio messages, can facilitate interactions.

Finally, although not focused on the senior audience, the study [27] presented guidelines for the design of messages based on focus group, interviews, and tests. The analysis results showed that users are receptive only to crucial messages, presented subtly, especially in the intervals of the schedules. Finally, in [28] and [29] television integrates Smart Home projects, which favor the access of the elderly to content and health-related care and assist in homework. Table 1 presents the sample of 15 articles mapped from databases, summing up the relevance that the notifications had within the studies found.

Table 1. Use of notifications to reduce the elderly's social isolation.

Ref	Goal	Strategy	Relevance
17	Connect people	Family reminders	High potential to stimulate interactions
18	Connect people	Phone calls alerts	High potential to connect generations
19	Connect people	Chatbot/gamification	High potential to connect people
1	Connect people	Facebook app adapted for television	High potential to promote online and offline interactions
20	Promoting health	Medical reminders	High potential to provide relevant information
21	Promoting health	Medical reminders	High potential to provide relevant information and improve health
22	Promoting health	Well-being reminders	Relevant to provide relevant information
24	Promoting health	Notifications to the family, reporting falls	TV was an important means of notifying families with agility
23	Promote learning	T-learning apps	High potential to promote learning
25	Evaluate the format/design	Study of relevant icons	Icons related to themes make it easy to understand messages
26	Evaluate the format/design	Testing a virtual assistant	Textual and verbal messages facilitated the understanding of the information
27	Evaluate the format/design	Study of the formats with better acceptance	Notifications are well accepted if they do not abruptly interrupt the contents
28	Smart Home system	Evaluation of TV in this context	Relevant to disclose the important reminders and assist in household chores

(continued)

Table 1. (*continued*)

Ref	Goal	Strategy	Relevance
29	Smart Home system	Evaluation of TV in this context	Relevant to disclose the important reminders and assist in household chores

4.2 Interviews with the Elderly

Consumption Habits of Television Content

Regarding the consumption of television content, all participants stated that they watch television every day. The daily TV watching average time is 6 h, reaching peaks of 17 h a day in some cases. "Turning on the tv is a habit. No matter what type of content, it's always on at home, whether it's to watch interesting programs or simply to make noise, disguising loneliness," said a 64-year-old participant.

About consumption habits and preferences, Fig. 3 shows the types of content that are most frequently consumed by respondents.

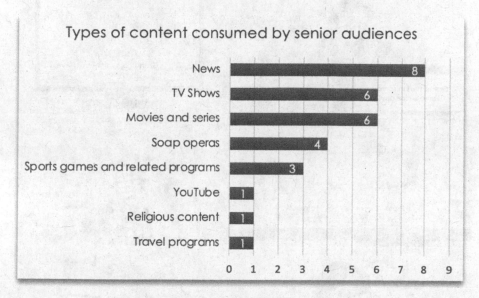

Fig. 3. Diversity of content consumed by the elderly.

Among all respondents, only 10% (2) stated that they have a Smart TV at home. However, one of the individuals said that he doesn't know how to use the resources. "I tend to use only the most traditional channels," said the 68-year-old. The other participant who claimed to own the device highlighted that he uses it daily to watch content available on YouTube. "I really like music videos and old songs. So, I decided to buy the device to watch what I'm interested in," commented the 69-year-old.

When asked if they consider television a kind of companion, especially in moments of solitude, only 20% (4) said they do not see the device in this way. The average age of these respondents is lower than the whole group average: 68.5. The other interviewees stated that they believe that television is a true companion and all seniors over 85 years of age stressed that "it would be very difficult to live without TV".

The relationship with the device is even more affective when it comes to the elderly who live alone, away from their families. "Time wouldn't pass if I didn't have television to watch. I don't know what I would do in my days," said a 90-year-old participant. "I'm alone all day. TV is a great companion for me. I wouldn't live without it," said an 87-year-old participant. "I watch all the shows and so my day goes faster," said a 95-year-old participant.

Notifications Built into iTV

The third part of the questionnaire sought to understand the group's perception of a possible display of notifications on the television screen. To contextualize the participants, especially those who are not so familiar with technology, a short-animated video was

Fig. 4. Example of message exchange with TV as an intermediary.

displayed (Fig. 4) giving an example of the use of notifications in a television context. In the animation created, a granddaughter sends a message (by mobile phone) to her grandmother, who is in front of the television. When notified, the older woman has the possibility to interact by pressing the "ok" button or reacting by voice. A heart emoji is automatically sent to the granddaughter, connecting the two generations in a more streamlined way.

Among the respondents, 25% (5) were resistant to the use of television notifications – these participants are 60, 66, 68, 77 and 87 years old. The 87-year-old approved the idea but was concerned about the data privacy displayed on TV. "Can more people see it? I'm afraid to expose my data", she said.

In general, participants aged 60, 66 and 68 who were resistant to the TV notifications, stated that it is because they already use the cell phone to send and receive messages and access social media apps. Therefore, they do not believe that the display of notifications on television would be a benefit. "On the contrary, it would hinder my experience. When I have the TV on, I want to disconnect from everything, enjoy that moment without interference", said the participant of 60 years. "I believe it's a good idea for older people with greater difficulty using electronic devices. But for me, it wouldn't make that much difference. Besides, I think the messages are very personal. I wouldn't want to share them with my daughter" said the 68-year-old.

Another participant (66 years old) who was opposed to the feature said that the feature could invade her privacy, since she would not like to see her messages displayed on television while you were with more people in the room. "You should have a possibility to configure the type of message you want to receive. Example: I didn't want my WhatsApp notifications to appear there," said.

For the individuals who approve messages on television (75% or 15 people in total), there was a consensus that this type of functionality is welcome because it is a well-known device to the elderly. That is, older people would easily send and receive messages. "I'm already used to television, and it would be very interesting to be able to receive messages, see photographs or inform myself through TV. Also, as I suffer from sight loss, it would be easier to read the messages on a larger screen," said a 95-year-old participant. In addition to this user, the screen size was mentioned by another participant, 90 years old. "On the phone everything is too small to read, I can hardly see the messages. On TV it would be a lot easier," she said. "I find it very interesting to receive messages on TV especially for elderly people who do not have access to technology and have difficulties. This kind of resource would add a lot to the lives of older people. They would feel welcomed," said a 63-year-old participant.

When asked about the type of content they would like to receive, among the 15 individuals who were receptive to notifications, all stated that they would like to have access to messages related to their family and friends. "What I would be most interested in receiving on television are pictures of my son to know what he has done and if he is well," said a 90-year-old participant. "I have a daughter who lives in another country and a son who works from Sunday to Sunday. I think it would be an easy way to be in touch with them," said an 87-year-old participant.

Still in the context of bringing people together, two participants (one of 69 and another of 81 years) said that it would be interesting to have the possibility of making video calls via television. "So, I could talk to my children and grandchildren more easily, besides being a bigger screen than the phone. I'd love to," said the 81-year-old.

Another feature well received by respondents was sending notifications to alert when the cell phone is ringing. Of the total number of people who approved the notifications, 80% (12) said they would like to be warned on television whenever a family member is calling on their mobile phone. "Often, I don't have my phone in my hands or don't listen it. It would be an asset," said an 81-year-old participant.

In addition, this same group of interviewees stated that it would be interesting to have an explanatory tutorial on the use of notifications on TV. "If it were in video format, I'd be easier to learn," commented an 88-year-old participant.

All participants were asked if they preferred to receive and respond to notifications using voice commands instead of typing responses. Among participants over 80 years of age (40% or 8 in total), the possibility was seen as an added facility. "I have difficulty typing, it takes me a long time to complete a sentence. I believe that talking, just by pressing a remote-control button, would be a good idea," said an 87-year-old participant. "I cannot type on the phone; the buttons are too small. The control ones are bigger, but I still think I'd have difficulties. So, I think talking instead of writing could be a good alternative," said a 90-year-old participant. Among participants under 80 years of age (60% or 12 in total), the possibility did not arouse much interest. "I'd rather type to talk. I'm not used to send voice messages through my cell phone and I think I wouldn't do the same on TV," commented a 69-year-old respondent.

In general, therefore, it can be verified that older interviewees were more receptive to the use of notifications in the television ecosystem. The highest rejection rate in the comparison between groups can be seen among participants aged 60 to 75 years (34%). It was possible to notice that, as age increases, the rate of rejection of notifications drops and, consequently, the acceptance rate grows (Fig. 5).

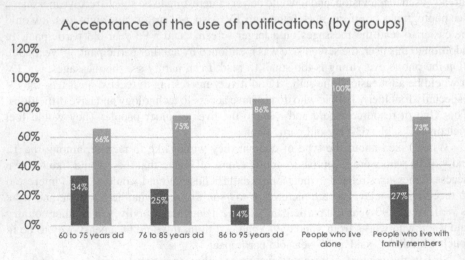

Fig. 5. Acceptance percentages by groups of interviewees.

The main reasons for the greater acceptance among older individuals were familiarity with the device, the size of messages that will be displayed on the screen (larger than on the mobile phone, which facilitates understanding) and the possibility of having easier access to content produced by their family members.

For respondents living alone, acceptance was the highest in the comparison between groups: 100%. For individuals living with other people (family members or partners), there was 27% rejection and 73% acceptance. These indicators show that respondents living alone are more receptive to the use of notifications in the television ecosystem. As we have seen before, these were also the ones that were most dependent on the device. Table 2 presents a compilation of some phrases separated by themes to facilitate understanding of user perception.

Table 2. Most significant phrases mentioned by users.

Main themes	Phrases mentioned by users
Acceptance	1. "It is an interesting resource, especially for older people. They would feel welcomed" (63-year-old participant) 2. "I don't think it's interesting because I see my notifications on my cell phone and when I go to watch TV I want to rest" (60-year-old participant) 3. "I really like the idea because television is something I've been using for many years. I think it would be easier" (90-year-old participant)
Proximity to family members	1. "It would be a way to be closer to my family, especially my grandchildren who live in another country" (87-year-old participant) 2. "I would love to be able to receive video calls also on television. I think it would be an interesting resource" (81-year-old participant)
Privacy	1. "I wouldn't want my messages to appear on the TV screen. I may be watching shows with other people and that would be a problem for me" (66-year-old participant) 2. "I don't think it would be interesting to see messages on TV. It's a kind of invasion of our privacy" (68-year-old participant) 3. "I would be afraid about privacy issues. Will more people have access to messages? It would have to be something well explained so that we can accept it or not" (87-year-old participant)

(*continued*)

Table 2. (*continued*)

Main themes	Phrases mentioned by users
Voice features	1. "I think it would be easier to say than to type. The buttons are small and could take longer to respond" (90-year-old participant)
Accessibility	1. "It would be a feature that would allow me to see the messages, since I have sight loss and cannot see text on the mobile" (95-year-old participant) 2. "I would like to see photos and messages on television because the TV screen is bigger than that of the mobile phone" (90-year-old participant)

In short, there is a variation in the perception of the elderly in relation to the use of notifications, greatly impacted by age and experiences.

5 Conclusions and Future Work

The analyzed studies pointed out the relevance of notifications in promoting interaction with other people, universes and themes, stimulating the search for information, the use of technological resources and health-related care. In addition, the prototypes presented contributed significantly to facilitating interactions with family and friends among the studies focusing on social isolation.

Articles focused essentially on health also contributed in a certain way to social integration since they present information that goes beyond that the elderly are accustomed to receiving, favoring the feeling of belonging to communities. Regarding the design of the messages, [19] and [26] showed that diversifying formats can contribute to the good acceptance of this audience. Voice interactions, for example, facilitated access to information sent by notifications and were still seen by the elderly as a companion, especially in studies involving the use of personal assistants. Notifications were also considered relevant when inserted in Smart Home systems, reminding the elderly about tasks to be done.

Therefore, this analysis has demonstrated the existence of relevant studies in this context. This survey also identified suitable methodological designs to discuss the theme, with analyses that suggested good practices and preferences of the elderly. Some of the studies presented here specifically addressed the contribution of TV in reducing social isolation, showing that the device can stimulate the contact of the elderly with other people, especially from different generations in the family. For this reason, it is understood the topic requires further studies, primarily involving tests done with real users in real contexts of usage. This mapping, therefore, was the first stage of this study, being crucial to identify aspects that were included in a questionnaire that a group of elderly has answered.

These interviews were conducted with elderly people between 60 and 95 years old to identify the following aspects considered relevant to the study: familiarity with technological resources, television consumption habits and perceptions regarding the usage of notifications in this ecosystem.

In general, a more positive reception was identified by the elderly who are over 80 years old or those who live with people of this age group. Notifications were mentioned as a mechanism capable of stimulating the exchange of messages between people of different generations. That is, since TV is already a known device of this audience, using it as an intermediary is an efficient way to promote interactions, especially among people who have difficulty using technological resources. Moreover, in general, television was pointed out by most users interviewed as a companion. Those over the age of 80, for example, said they "wouldn't know what their lives would be like without TV." Therefore, integrating new features into the device, such as notifications, proved to be a consistent way to reduce loneliness rates, especially among those who are older and live alone.

In addition to the results of the literature review, the data from the interviews conducted with the group of elderly also contributed to the identification of relevant factors that will support the creation of scenarios to be tested, throughout the work, with the elderly. These scenarios aim to evaluate the User Experience (UX) related to the use of notifications in the television ecosystem and show their potential to personalize information and promote interactions between individuals.

The results of these tests will be presented in future works and support the development of a prototype to be evaluated by the senior public and their relatives or caregivers. The prototype mentioned here aims to test the use of notifications, with real users, within the television ecosystem.

In a way, this study identifies that the television ecosystem has great potential to connect generations and promote exchanges between individuals of different ages, which is a gain for the elderly, since historically they have more difficulties related to the use of electronic devices. That is, TV, besides being considered a companion can contribute effectively to reduce the rates of loneliness.

References

1. Coelho, J., Rito, F., Duarte, C.: "You, me & TV"—fighting social isolation of older adults with Facebook, TV and multimodality. Int. J. Hum. Comput. Stud. **98**, 38–50 (2017)
2. Conroy, K., Krishnan, S., Mittelstaedt, S., Patel, S.: Technological advancements to address elderly loneliness: practical considerations and community resilience implications for COVID-19 pandemic. Work. Older People **24**, 257–264 (2020)
3. Seifert, A.: The digital exclusion of older adults during the COVID-19 pandemic. J. Gerontol. Soc. Work **63**, 674–676 (2020)
4. Vaportzis, E., Martin, M., Gow, A.J.: A tablet for healthy ageing: the effect of a tablet computer training intervention on cognitive abilities in older adults. Am. J. Geriatr. Psychiatry **25**, 841–851 (2017)
5. Zhang, B., Sundar, S.: Proactive vs. reactive personalization: can customization of privacy enhance user experience? Int. J. Hum. Comput. Stud. **128**, 86–99 (2019)
6. Meurisch, C., et al.: Exploring user expectations of proactive AI systems. In: Proceedings of the ACM on Interactive, Mobile, Wearable and Ubiquitous Technologies (2019)

7. Figueroa, A., Aguilera, A.: The need for a mental health technology revolution in the COVID-19 pandemic. Front. Psych. **11**, 523 (2020)
8. CDC Homepage. https://www.cdc.gov/nchs/nvss/vsrr/covid_weekly/index.htm. Accessed 03 Oct 2021
9. GNR Homepage. https://www.gnr.pt/MVC_GNR/Recortes/Details/15479. Accessed 07 Oct 2021
10. Medium Homepage. https://medium.com/@nicoleellison/stocking-the-social-pantry-a-rec ipe-for-getting-from-social-distancing-to-distant-socializing-6e2a21133858. Accessed 07 Oct 2021
11. Iqbal, T., Horvitz, E.: Notifications and awareness: a field study of alert usage and preferences. In: Proceedings of the ACM Conference on Computer Supported Cooperative Work, CSCW, pp. 27–30 (2010)
12. Gameiro, F.: Platform of Advertising and Push Notifications for Mobile Apps, 112. https:// estudogeral.sib.uc.pt/bitstream/10316/35671/1/PlatformofAdvertisingandPushNotificatio nsforMobileApps.pdf
13. Mehrotra, A., Pejovic, V., Vermeulen, J., Hendley, R., Musolesi, M.: My phone and me: understanding people's receptivity to mobile notification. In: CHI Conference on Human Factors in Computing Systems, vol. 16, pp. 1021–1032 (2016)
14. Wheatley, D., Ferrer-Conill, R.: The temporal nature of mobile push notification alerts: a study of European news outlets' dissemination patterns. Digit. J. **9**(6), 694–714 (2021)
15. Silva, A., Leithardt, Q., Rolim, O., González, V., Geyer, R., Silva, S.: Priser: managing notification in multiples devices with data privacy support. Sensors **19**(14), 1–18 (2019)
16. Moher, D., et al.: Preferred reporting items for systematic reviews and meta-analyses: the PRISMA statement. PLoS Med. **6**, e1000097 (2009)
17. Voit, A., Weber, D., Stowell, E., Henze, N.: Caloo: an ambient pervasive smart calendar to support aging in place. In: ACM International Conference Proceeding Series, pp. 25–30 (2017)
18. Hong, T., Su, Y., Lee, H., Hsieh, C., Chiu, J.: VisualLink: strengthening the connection between hearing-impaired elderly and their family. In: Conference on Human Factors in Computing Systems, pp. 67–73 (2017)
19. Valtolina, S., Hu, L.: Charlie: a chatbot to improve the elderly quality of life and to make them more active to fight their sense of loneliness. In: ACM International Conference Proceeding Series (2021)
20. Santana-Mancilla, C., Anido-Rifón, E.: iTVCare: a home care system for the elderly through interactive television. In: Avances En Interacción Humano-Computadora, vol. 1, p. 92 (2018)
21. Bureš, V., Mikulecká, J., Ponce, D.: Digital television as a usable platform for enhancement of learning possibilities for the elderly. SAGE Open **7**(2), 1–9 (2017)
22. Santana-Mancilla, C., Anido-Rifón, E., Contreras-Castillo, J.: Designing for social iTV: improving the shared experience of home care systems. In: ACM International Conference Proceeding Series, pp. 1–4 (2019)
23. Silva, T., Campelo, D., Caravau, H., de Abreu, J.F.: Delivering information of general interest through interactive television: a taxonomy of assistance services for the Portuguese elderly. In: Röcker, C., O'Donoghue, J., Ziefle, M., Maciaszek, L., Molloy, W. (eds.) ICT4AWE 2017. CCIS, vol. 869, pp. 191–208. Springer, Cham (2018). https://doi.org/10.1007/978-3-319-93644-4_10
24. Watanapa, B., Patsadu, O., Dajpratham, P., Nukoolkit, C.: Post-fall intelligence supporting fall severity diagnosis using kinect sensor. Appl. Comput. Intell. Soft Comput. **2018**, 1–15 (2018)
25. Silva, T., Caravau, H., Reis, L., Almeida, P.: Iconography's development for a seniors' iTV informative platform. Procedia Comput. Sci. **121**, 576–583 (2017)

26. Rojc, M., Mlakar, I., Kačič, Z.: The TTS-driven affective embodied conversational agent EVA, based on a novel conversational-behavior generation algorithm. Eng. Appl. Artif. Intell. **57**, 80–104 (2017)
27. Weber, D., Mayer, S., Voit, A., Fierro, R.V., Henze, N.: Design guidelines for notifications on smart TVs. In: TVX 2016 - Proceedings of the ACM International Conference on Interactive Experiences for TV and Online Video, pp. 13–24 (2016)
28. Mostafa, S.A., Gunasekaran, S.S., Mustapha, A., Mohammed, M.A., Abduallah, W.M.: Modelling an adjustable autonomous multi-agent Internet of Things system for elderly smart home. In: Ayaz, H. (ed.) AHFE 2019. AISC, vol. 953, pp. 301–311. Springer, Cham (2020). https://doi.org/10.1007/978-3-030-20473-0_29
29. Ponce, S., et al.: Wearable sensors and domotic environment for elderly people. In: Lhotska, L., Sukupova, L., Lacković, I., Ibbott, G.S. (eds.) World Congress on Medical Physics and Biomedical Engineering 2018. IP, vol. 68/3, pp. 195–200. Springer, Singapore (2019). https://doi.org/10.1007/978-981-10-9023-3_35
30. Almeida, P., Abreu, J., Silva, T., Duro, L., Aresta, M., Oliveira, R.: Notification mechanisms in second-screen scenarios towards a balanced user experience. In: Proceedings of the 2015 7th International Conference on Intelligent Technologies for Interactive Entertainment (2015)
31. Silva, T., Almeida, P., Cardoso, B., Oliveira, R., Cunha, A., Ribeiro, C.: Smartly: a TV companion app to deliver discount coupons. In: Abásolo, M.J., Kulesza, R., Pina Amargós, J.D. (eds.) jAUTI 2019. CCIS, vol. 1202, pp. 53–66. Springer, Cham (2020). https://doi.org/10.1007/978-3-030-56574-9_4

Interaction Techniques and Accessibility

Real-Time Emotion Recognition Through Video Conference and Streaming

Nancy Paredes[1,2](✉), Eduardo Caicedo Bravo[2], and Bladimir Bacca[2]

[1] WiCOM-Energy Research Group, Universidad de Las Fuerzas Armadas ESPE, Sangolquí, Ecuador
nancy.paredes@correounivalle.edu.co
[2] PSI-Sistemas de Percepción Inteligentes, Universidad del Valle, Cali, Colombia
{eduardo.caicedo,bladimir.bacca}@correounivalle.edu.co

Abstract. The Covid-19 pandemic changed the course of activities, both work and education in the world, migrating to the requirement of virtual platforms and videoconferencing tools, such as Zoom, Google Meet, Jitsi Meet, among others. This generated a globalized and digital culture of learning, activities in congresses, and even business meetings using videoconferences. This new scenario creates uncertainty, especially in educators, due to the level of attention they are receiving from students through virtual classes and other scenarios where they want to evaluate the emotions created in the people who receive them information virtual written description intended to provide factual informationally. For this reason, to support different video conferencing platforms or other audiovisual media, a tool is presented that captures video in real-time. It automatically recognizes the emotions expressed by people using deep learning tools, happiness, sadness, surprise, anger, fear, disgust, and neutral emotions. The initial training and validation system is based on the CK+ Dataset that contains images distributed by emotions. This tool was developed for the WEB in Python Flask, which in addition to automatic recognition in real-time, generates statistics of the emotions of the people evaluated with 75% accuracy. To validate the tool, videoconferencing programs were used, the emotions of a group of students were evaluated, and open videos were available online on YouTube. With this study, it was possible to re-know the emotions of the people who attended the class, which allows the teacher to take measures if the students do not carry out the planned activities.

Keywords: Emotions · Videoconferences · *Deep learning* · Python · Flask

1 Introduction

Currently, virtual environments have become the means through which many people carry out their daily activities; this has deepened since the end of 2019 with the arrival of the COVID-19 pandemic, which forced us to change our work environments, educational, recreational activities, etc. by virtual environments managed in the vast majority through videoconferences, teleworking, tele education, etc.

© Springer Nature Switzerland AG 2022
M. J. Abásolo and G. F. Olmedo Cifuentes (Eds.): jAUTI 2021, CCIS 1597, pp. 39–52, 2022.
https://doi.org/10.1007/978-3-031-22210-8_3

Within this context, emotions have played a fundamental role in coping with the changes those human beings have suffered in the last two years; their ability to adapt to new and unknown circumstances has put them to the test, for which it is necessary to analyze how people have adapted to this and how they interact in these new environments; emotions being a door to understand these processes of everyone.

Daily activity is education, in which teachers must have the ability to identify the facial expressions shown by their students as a source of feedback within the teaching-learning process, considering that the face allows us to identify various emotional aspects of the person. This proposal proposes the implementation of algorithms based on artificial intelligence, which identifies emotions in any situation through virtual environments.

This proposal presents in point 2 a compilation of works related to the recognition of emotions studied from the psychological point of view and using artificial intelligence; in point 3, it shows the methodology applied for the tool's implementation; in point 4, the results are presented; and finally, in point 5, a perspective of new research based on this presented work.

2   Related Work

The analysis of emotions in real-time in virtual environments is a current problem, which has been approached from different aspects; several of these detection methods are linked to physiological changes in people [1, 2] for example, there are several applications with real-time face detection for emotion recognition based on artificial intelligence [3], mainly used to measure the degree of user satisfaction. Some studies develop web applications to recognize emotions in neuromarketing, managing to develop open systems, using the webcam when accessing the content, constituting a starting point to personalize internet marketing services in real-time [4]; in many of these studies, electroencephalograms have been used on magnetic resonance imaging-based on video advertisements, eye-tracking techniques, skin conductance recording, heart rate monitoring, facial mapping have also been used [5].

Other studies have allowed space for virtual characters to become popular, which is why facial expression recognition plays an important role in virtual assistants, online video games, security systems, video conferencing, virtual reality, and online classes. Lines based on a multi-block deep convolutional neural network (DCNN) model to recognize the facial emotions of stylized virtual characters [6].

In education, due to the COVID 19 pandemic, all countries had to change the modality of face-to-face studies to virtual, specifically in Ecuador; a plan was established, which had guidelines for the prioritized curriculum, but an educational program was also designed, available on television and rural community radios [7], oriented especially to schools in remote areas, but in urban areas priority was given to interactive virtual classes with the teacher. However, in this case, social inequality was verified where most low-income students did not have a secure internet connection [8].

The situations that have arisen due to the pandemic force educators to analyze the emotional aspect of students; this has represented a great challenge, especially in synchronous classes, since the identification of the emotional part constitutes feedback for teachers to make improvements on the fly, that is, in real-time, so as not to lose the attention of the students [9].

Emotions play an essential role in student learning and performance. They control the student's attention, affect their motivation to learn, and influence their self-regulation of learning [10]. Mega mentions that self-regulated learning and motivation mediate the effects of emotions on academic performance [11].

Positive emotions affect academic performance when they are mediated by self-regulation of learning and motivation. In recent years, deep learning algorithms have dominated the field of facial recognition through convolutional neural networks, which are deep learning architectures [10].

Studies have been carried out to understand the emotions involved in online learning and the emotional states that these processes generate from a perspective that allows exploring ways to understand the relationships between emotions, learning, and social values in resources, educational content, and environment ambient. Goetz (2005) points out the scant attention that emotions have received in educational processes during the 20th century, with two notable exceptions: the study of anxiety related to evaluation and performance (exams, tests, etc.) and the study of the relationship between emotion and motivation related to academic success and failure (guilt, pride, etc.). In his analysis, Pekrun acknowledges how little knowledge we still have about the occurrence, frequency, and phenomenology of emotions in different learning environments, especially in online learning [12].

In 2016, a face identification system was proposed for e-learning students applying Viola-Jones, dynamically capturing the emotions shown in response to the conference [13].

In 2019, a system made with convolution networks was presented, training the FER 2013 dataset and using a transfer technique based on the VGG16 architecture, allowing the recognition accuracy to be improved to 85% [14]. In the year 2020, studies based on artificial intelligence methods for online learning allowed to be a door to analyze the well-being of attendees based on ATT-LSTM (*Attention-based - Long Short-Term Memory*) [15] and A-CNN (*Annularly Convolutional Neural Networks*) with an accuracy of 88.62% and 71.12% respectively, also used as a real-time feedback system to obtain facial expressions from students and judge the didactic effect through the changes in your face [16].

3 Methodology

In general, the designed system presents a structure with the interface associated with a WEB page of the HTML type that presents the options of video detection through a WEB camera for the cases that the classes are in person or video detection of video-conferences in the case that they are virtual classes. In order to capture the video of any videoconferencing tool, a mirror-type capture of the region of the screen that contains the information of any video being played was made. The selected region is processed through specific libraries for Python, which will be described later, which will allow to detection of the edges of the face and then discrimination its parts and detect emotions through a deep learning process. For online classes, the teacher can pin the video they want to assess from the student's camera. By detecting any video, the system can work with any multimedia element, such as streaming or television content, considering that both the software and hardware of current televisions already have built-in streaming systems.

A web application was implemented through the Flask Framework developed in Python [17], which uses the WSGI server (Web Server Gateway Interface). The Web application, being developed in Python, allows the direct incorporation of image processing and facial recognition tools through OpenCV and Deep Learning tools using Keras and Tensorflow libraries. Table 1 describes the elements used for the design of the Web application.

Table 1. Web application design elements.

Elements	Archive	Description
Flask methods	app.py	It processes all the routes of the WEB application
	capture.py	Processes the emotion recognition system of faces captured in Video Conferences and videos in general
	webcam.py	Processes the emotion recognition system of faces captured by the WEB camera
Templates	Index.html	Main HTML page that is associated with app.py
	Capture.html	HTML page that starts capturing faces in videos and displays the emotion recognition result in real-time
	Webcam.html	HTML page that starts capturing faces from the WEB camera and displays the emotion recognition result in real-time
	Contacto.hmtl	HTML page with contact information for the project developers
Static resources	style.css	CSS file to define styles
	Images	Images of the web application
Resources for emotion recognition	haarcascade_frontalface_default.xml	Pre-trained classifiers for face recognition based on Viola-Jones algorithm included in OpenCV

(continued)

Table 1. (*continued*)

Elements	Archive	Description
	Trained.hdf5	Deep Learning architecture trained to classify emotions using Keras and Tensorflow
Statistical registration of data and images	XLS file with the record of detected emotions	Registered data of emotions detected during the evaluation time, based on the openpyxl library for Python
	Captured images	Images of captured faces
	Images with emotions detected	Images of faces captured with emotion framed

Resources for Emotion Recognition

Initially, the OpenCV library was used, which contains the pre-trained classifier for face recognition, which includes the Viola-Jones algorithm, based on the extraction of features from what is known as integral images through masks of Haar and cascade of Boosting classifiers [18, 19]. Figure 1 shows an example of a face, eye, nose, and mouth recognition using the Viola-Jones algorithm.

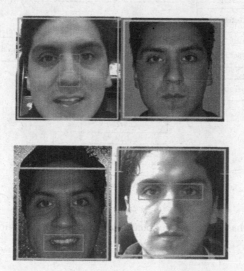

Fig. 1. Viola-Jones, recognition of face, eyes, nose, and mouth.

In [20, 21], the authors propose a model based on convolutional neural networks to classify emotions in real-time. The architecture used is presented in Fig. 2, which is structured in an mini-Xception architecture, which combines separate modules of 2D convolutional networks. The architecture was trained with an ADAM-type optimizer and a Global Average Pooling stage that completely removes the connected layers.

In [20, 21], the architecture was trained and validated with the FER2013 DataSet [22], which contains 35887 images classified by anger, disgust, fear, happiness, sadness, surprise, and neutral expressions. In previous research, this database was analyzed, obtaining 66% accuracy [23]. In our case, we additionally validate the architecture with the CK+ DataSet [24], with 45 images of expressions of anger, 49 of disgust, 25 of fear, 69 of joy, 28 of sadness, 83 of surprise, and 93 of neutrality. In Fig. 3, you can see an example of the images of faces in this dataset.

The trained model was saved in a file in "hdf5" format to be used in Python through Keras in the images of the faces captured in the videos.

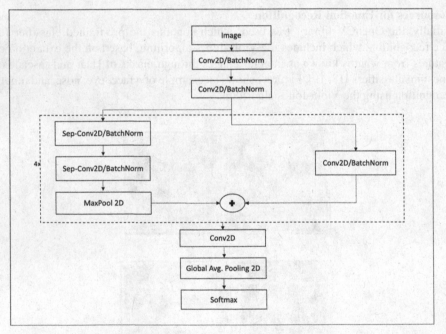

Fig. 2. Model-based on convolutional neural networks for emotion recognition.

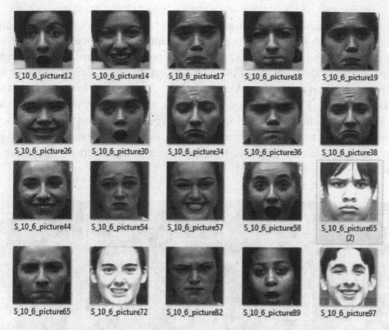

Fig. 3. Example of CK+ DataSet.

Statistical Registration of Data and Images

For each video session, an XLS file was created that records every 0.25 s the probabilities obtained by the classification model and the detected emotion that presents the highest probability (Fig. 4), for which the openpyxl library was used for Python. The sum of the probabilities gives the value of one, and the detected emotion's decision will be the one with the highest probability.

	A	B	C	D	E	F	G	H	I
1	Hora	Emoción	P_enojo	P_asco	P_miedo	P_felicidad	P_tristeza	P_sopresa	P_neutral
2	17:56:56	Neutral	0,135738	0,008862	0,130974	0,064009	0,107063	0,009134	0,544219
3	17:56:57	Neutral	0,144155	0,001999	0,151745	0,129355	0,072454	0,019408	0,480884
4	17:56:57	Neutral	0,115589	0,002455	0,216137	0,185316	0,101324	0,017073	0,362106
5	17:56:57	Neutral	0,062138	0,000733	0,142403	0,206664	0,082509	0,011497	0,494056
6	17:56:58	Neutral	0,062813	0,00153	0,098786	0,178118	0,113429	0,008889	0,536435
7	17:56:58	Neutral	0,096142	0,001127	0,112632	0,158862	0,072731	0,011611	0,546897
8	17:56:59	Neutral	0,104881	0,003339	0,204298	0,140678	0,094034	0,010086	0,442684
9	17:56:59	Feliz	0,107794	0,001511	0,090196	0,384895	0,082658	0,006519	0,326426
10	17:56:59	Neutral	0,092814	0,003587	0,096441	0,200133	0,11253	0,006554	0,487942
11	17:57:00	Neutral	0,131012	0,003152	0,107807	0,247138	0,121901	0,007147	0,381843
12	17:57:00	Neutral	0,140462	0,004086	0,123075	0,275106	0,081765	0,011114	0,364392
13	17:57:01	Neutral	0,142306	0,007341	0,118481	0,13311	0,091083	0,007037	0,500643
14	17:57:01	Neutral	0,151994	0,006045	0,10072	0,124392	0,10684	0,009833	0,500175
15	17:57:01	Neutral	0,167721	0,005191	0,112857	0,203328	0,063787	0,008817	0,438299
16	17:57:02	Neutral	0,144237	0,005417	0,081557	0,179523	0,091649	0,008639	0,488979
17	17:57:02	Neutral	0,083371	0,004023	0,082214	0,139419	0,094667	0,003942	0,592365
18	17:57:26	Feliz	0,114876	0,008791	0,091867	0,440574	0,070609	0,011912	0,26137
19	17:57:27	Feliz	0,081862	0,02051	0,160663	0,278297	0,13341	0,064487	0,260772

Fig. 4. Example of record in XLS file.

Additionally, the images of the original faces are saved (Fig. 5a), and with the emotion detected (Fig. 5b) with their respective date, time, and sequence, using OpenCV tools to evaluate the model and create new DataSets for future system training. The registered images are named with the name of the XLS file and the time of registration in the file.

For this application to be integrated into a television, the emotion recognition system will be embedded in a mini PC that would work as a decoder, obtaining the signals through the camera while transmitting the audio and video signal. The processed data will be based on each transmitted frame to evaluate the respective emotion. The emotion that gets the highest probability will be the one that is displayed on the screen as the identified emotion.

(a)   Example of saved images from video captures.

(b)   Example of images saved with face and emotion recognition.

Fig. 5. Statistical registration of data and images.

User Interface

The user interface was designed so that its use is intuitive, and in the same way, it allows obtaining information that will be constantly stored, as shown in Fig. 6.

The tool is automatically enabled through WEB design programming built on the Flask Framework, which directly loads Python libraries.

The configuration tools allow you to configure the internal or external webcam or set the screen capture mode, dividing it into two regions, one where the videoconference or streaming to be evaluated is observed and the second with a mirror of the video, where the recognition is processed face and emotions.

The data captured and processed are saved in images, both the original and the processed ones, where the emotion shown is recognized. A statistic is also kept by time, which is saved in Excel format, which records the name of the processed image with all the possible probabilities of each emotion. Although it is most likely tagged with emotion, all of this information is useful for further training to improve the precision and accuracy of the tool designed for deep learning. The captures are associated in folders and recorded with the date, time, and sequence number of the processed frame, which generates a new data set.

The sample of results is done graphically, presenting in the video a box on the face of the person evaluated and labeling the emotion, which allows the end user to observe the emotions detected in the video in real-time.

To be integrated into a television, the emotion recognition system will be embedded in a mini PC that would function as a decoder, obtaining the signals through the camera while transmitting the audio and video signal. The processed data will be based on each transmitted frame to assess the respective emotion. The emotion that gets the highest probability will be the one that is displayed on the screen as the identified emotion.

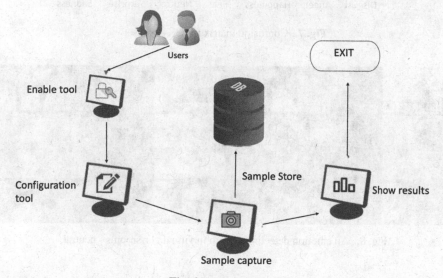

Fig. 6. User interface

4   Results

The deep learning training system shows us the accuracy results presented in the confusion matrix of Fig. 7, where a total accuracy of 75% was achieved, with happiness at 97.1%, surprise at 83.1%, and neutral at 82.8%. In contrast, sadness, anger, and disgust max out at 60%, and fear has less than 44% accuracy.

Classifier output	Disgust	Anger	Happiness	Fear	Neutral	Surprise	Sadness	
Disgust	27 6.9%	0 0.0%	0 0.0%	0 0.0%	0 0.0%	0 0.0%	0 0.0%	100% 0.0%
Anger	14 3.6%	27 6.9%	0 0.0%	4 1.0%	0 0.0%	5 1.3%	4 1.0%	51.9 % 48.15%
Happiness	1 0.3%	3 0.8%	67 17.1%	1 0.3%	0 0.0%	0 0.0%	0 0.0%	93.1 % 6.9%
Fear	2 0.5%	5 1.3%	0 0.0%	11 2.8%	12 3.1%	6 1.5%	5 1.3%	26.8% 73.2%
Neutral	1 0.3%	2 0.5%	2 0.5%	2 0.5%	77 19.6%	5 1.3%	3 0.8%	83.7 % 16.3%
Surprise	1 0.3%	2 0.5%	0 0.0%	2 0.5%	1 0.3%	69 17.6%	0 0.0%	92.0% 8.0%
Sadness	1 0.3%	6 1.5%	0 0.0%	5 1.3%	3 0.8%	0 0.0%	16 4.1%	48.5% 51.5%
	55.1% 44.9%	60.0% 40.0%	97.1% 2.9%	44.0% 56.0%	82.8% 17.2%	83.1% 16.9%	57.1% 42.9%	75.0% 25.0%
	Disgust	Anger	Happiness	Fear	Neutral	Surprise	Sadness	

Fig. 7. Confusion matrix for CK+ dataset

Fig. 8. An emotion detection system in virtual classrooms - neutral.

To validate the tool, 12 university students collaborated, and experiments were carried out in a virtual educational environment to capture in real time the emotions they show in a synchronous class. Figure 8 shows the screen of the videoconferencing system used for that class with the attending students. First, the system detects the face of the student to be analyzed and places it in a box, and immediately begins to detect the emotion shown by that person who attends the virtual classroom. This process can be carried out with each of the videoconference attendees who have your webcam; Fig. 9 shows that when you want to lock the screen on a particular student to analyze only that person, the sequence of emotions shown in the synchronous session is recognized. These emotions represent an input to define a strategy that allows the teacher to detect if interest is lost or the student shows negative emotions such as anger, sadness, etc. In these situations, the teacher must apply strategies that capture the interest and attention of the students attending the class to obtain the expected learning results.

Another way to validate was through videos found on the network; as shown in Fig. 10, a YouTube video captured in real-time.

When working with television content, the emotion recognition system works in the same way as with any content that arrives via streaming, from the capture and recognition of the video.

On the other hand, there is an additional proposal to recognize the emotions of the user who watches television programming, which would work with the same application proposed in this article, supported by the cameras that televisions already have integrated for intelligent interactive applications or also the project can be configured on a mini PC with a WEB camera and directly use the Python libraries for emotion recognition, proposed and implemented in this article.

Fig. 9. Recognition of emotions in virtual classrooms of a specific person – Happiness (*Feliz* in spanhish).

Fig. 10. Detection of emotions through YouTube video.

5 Discussion and Conclusions

In this proposal, an emotion recognition tool was presented in virtual environments, through any platform used for videoconferences or other audiovisual media, fulfilling the objective of supporting activities where the interaction of two or more people can be improved through recognition and interpretation of the emotions of the interlocutors. This experience allows you to contribute to the results of the activities carried out virtually to capture the attention of the people with whom you interact to achieve the expected result in the proposed activity.

The average accuracy of 75% was obtained from the validation of the deep learning training system, where the emotion of happiness was the emotion with the highest accuracy at 97.5%.

This work constitutes a starting point to carry out in future research an in-depth study of interactive systems in the classroom, the recognition of emotions in videos of television productions, such as newscasts, or the contribution to neuromarketing evaluations, among others. The interface developed in Python can be included in specialized hardware to operate with videos, such as TV-Box, cell phones, SDR, micro-PC, or development boards such as Raspberry Pi. The classifier used in this work also constitutes a starting point for new research in other areas of human activities to improve communication and appropriate assistance from an analysis based on the understanding of their emotions.

The Python language allowed the trained system to be processed on multiple platforms, including hardware, mobile phones, or television applications.

The images captured from the video frames were recorded at the same time, where the detection of the face with the label of the detected emotion is found, which will allow an additional validation of the recognition algorithm and, at the same time, allows to have more samples of the set of data from people who show emotions in real situations, that is, in uncontrolled environments, which can be used for new training with deep learning and improve the accuracy in the evaluation of emotions. In this case, it is essential to mention that the training was carried out only with the data from the CK+ DataSet.

If we have control of the WEB camera, the brightness and contrast play an essential role since the light should not be exceeded, and the image should not be dark either. In both cases, the information is not readable, and when going through the filtering stage, important features could not be extracted. That is why it must be in a neutral place, where it is recommended that the light intensity is, on average, 300 lx.

References

1. Bundele, M., Banerjee, R.: Detection of fatigue of vehicular driver using skin conductance and oximetry pulse: a neural network approach. In: iiWAS2009 - The 11th International Conference on Information Integration and Web-based Applications and Services, 2009, pp. 739–744 (2009). https://doi.org/10.1145/1806338.1806478
2. Li, C., Xu, C., Feng, Z.: Analysis of physiological for emotion recognition with IRS model. Neurocomputing **178**, 103–111 (2015). https://doi.org/10.1016/j.neucom.2015.07.112
3. Londoño-Osorio, V., Marín-Pineda, J., Zuluaga, A., Isabel, E.: Introducción a la Visión Artificial mediante Prácticas de Laboratorio Diseñadas en Matlab. TecnoLógicas, pp. 591–603 (2013). https://doi.org/10.22430/22565337.350
4. Filipović, F., Baljak, L., Naumović, T., Labus, A., Bogdanović, Z.: Developing a web application for recognizing emotions in neuromarketing. In: Rocha, Á., Reis, J.L., Peter, M.K., Bogdanović, Z. (eds.) Marketing and Smart Technologies. SIST, vol. 167, pp. 297–308. Springer, Singapore (2020). https://doi.org/10.1007/978-981-15-1564-4_28
5. Rawnaque, F.S., et al.: Technological advancements and opportunities in neuromarketing: a systematic review. Brain Inform. **7**(1), 1–19 (2020). https://doi.org/10.1186/s40708-020-00109-x
6. Chirra, V.R.R., Uyyala, S.R., Kolli, V.K.K.: Virtual facial expression recognition using deep CNN with ensemble learning. J. Ambient. Intell. Humaniz. Comput. **12**(12), 10581–10599 (2021). https://doi.org/10.1007/s12652-020-02866-3
7. Mateus, J.-C., Andrada, P., González-Cabrera, C., Ugalde, C., Novomisky, S.: Teachers' perspectives for a critical agenda in media education post COVID-19. A comparative study in Latin America. Comunicar **30**(70), 9–19 (2022). https://doi.org/10.3916/C70-2022-01
8. Vivanco-Saraguro, A.: Teleducación en tiempos de COVID-19: brechas de desigualdad. CienciAmérica **9**, 166–175 (2020). https://doi.org/10.33210/ca.v9i2.307
9. Rebollo-Catalan, A., Pérez, R., Sánchez, R.B., Buzón-García, O., Caro, L.: Las emociones en el aprendizaje online. Relieve: Revista Electrónica de Investigación y Evaluación Educativa **14**, 1–23 (2014). https://doi.org/10.7203/relieve.14.1.4201, ISSN 1134-4032
10. El Hammoumi, O., Benmarrakchi, F., Ouherrou, N., El Kafi, J., El Hore, A.: Emotion recognition in e-learning systems. In: 2018 6th International Conference on Multimedia Computing and Systems (ICMCS), pp. 1–6 (2018). https://doi.org/10.1109/ICMCS.2018.8525872
11. Mega, C., Ronconi, L., De Beni, R.: What makes a good student? How emotions, self-regulated learning, and motivation contribute to academic achievement. J. Educ. Psychol. **106**(1), 121–131 (2014). https://doi.org/10.1037/a0033546
12. Goetz, T., Frenzel, A. Pekrun, R., Hall, N.: Emotional intelligence in the context of learning and achievement. In: Schulze, R., Roberts, R.D. (eds.) Emotional Intelligence: An international Handbook, pp. 233–253. Hogrefe & Huber Publishers, Cambridge (2005). ISBN 0-88937-283-7
13. Krithika, L., Lakshmi, G.G.: Student emotion recognition system (SERS) for e-learning improvement based on learner concentration metric. Procedia Comput. Sci. **85**, 767–776 (2016). https://doi.org/10.1016/j.procs.2016.05.264
14. Sharma, A., Mansotra, V.: Deep learning based student emotion recognition from facial expressions in classrooms. Int. J. Eng. Adv. Technol. **8**(6), 4691–4699 (2019). https://doi.org/10.35940/ijeat.F9170.088619

15. Darabian, H., et al.: Detecting cryptomining malware: a deep learning approach for static and dynamic analysis. J. Grid Comput. **18**(2), 293–303 (2020). https://doi.org/10.1007/s10723-020-09510-6

16. Jain, A., Sah, H.: Student's feedback by emotion and speech recognition through deep learning. In: Proceedings - IEEE 2021 International Conference on Computing, Communication, and Intelligent Systems, ICCCIS 2021, pp. 442–447 (2021). https://doi.org/10.1109/ICCCIS 51004.2021.9397145

17. Welcome to Flask—Flask Documentation (2.1.x). https://flask.palletsprojects.com/en/2.1.x/. Accessed 25 Apr 2022

18. Al-Tuwaijari, J., Shaker, S.: Face detection system based viola-jones algorithm. In: Proceedings of the 6th International Engineering Conference "Sustainable Technology and Development", IEC 2020, pp. 211–215 (2020). https://doi.org/10.1109/IEC49899.2020.912 2927

19. Shah, R.: Face mask detection using convolution neural network. Computer Vision and Pattern Recognition (cs.CV); Image and Video Processing (eess.IV) (2021). https://doi.org/10.48550/ arXiv.2106.05728

20. Arriaga, O., Plöger, P.G., Valdenegro, M.: Real-time convolutional neural networks for emotion and gender classification. In: European Symposium on Artificial Neural Networks, Computational Intelligence and Machine Learning, pp. 221–226 (2019)

21. Gogate, U., Parate, A., Sah, S., Narayanan, S.: Real time emotion recognition and gender classification. In: Proceedings of the 2020 International Conference on Smart Innovations in Design, Environment, Management, Planning and Computing, ICSIDEMPC 2020, pp. 138–143 (2020). https://doi.org/10.1109/ICSIDEMPC49020.2020.9299633

22. Goodfellow, I.J., et al.: Challenges in representation learning: a report on three machine learning contests. In: Lee, M., Hirose, A., Hou, Z.-G., Kil, R.M. (eds.) ICONIP 2013. LNCS, vol. 8228, pp. 117–124. Springer, Heidelberg (2013). https://doi.org/10.1007/978-3-642-42051-1_16

23. Sun, L., Ge, C., Zhong, Y.: Design and implementation of face emotion recognition system based on CNN Mini_Xception frameworks. J. Phys. Conf. Ser. **2010**, 012123 (2021). https:// doi.org/10.1088/1742-6596/2010/1/012123

24. Lucey, P., Cohn, J.F., Kanade, T., Saragih, J., Ambadar, Z., Matthews, I.: The extended Cohn-Kanade dataset (CK+): a complete dataset for action unit and emotion-specified expression. In: 2010 IEEE Computer Society Conference on Computer Vision and Pattern Recognition - Workshops, CVPRW 2010, pp. 94–101 (2010). https://doi.org/10.1109/CVPRW.2010.554 3262

Emotional Meta-annotation of Educational Videos. A Review of Emotional Database Characterization

Gustavo J. Astudillo[1]([✉]) [iD], Cecilia V. Sanz[2] [iD], and Sandra Baldassarri[3] [iD]

[1] National University of La Pampa, La Pampa, Argentina
astudillo@exactas.unlpam.edu.ar
[2] National University of La Plata, Buenos Aires, Argentina
[3] University of Zaragoza, Aragón, Spain

Abstract. Publishing and using videos in educational activities, both formal and informal contexts, is becoming more frequent. This requires metadata that allows both computer systems and users to manage this particular type of educational resource. In previous research by the authors, a growing interest in the use of emotions to enrich the possibilities of e-learning systems was discussed, and a lack of standards for the emotional meta-annotation of educational videos was identified. This set the grounds for further investigation. In this article, a first analysis of a group of databases that host emotionally tagged videos is presented. The research focuses on reviewing how the characterization of these databases is carried out in search of identifying meta-annotated elements, specifically concerning emotions. Based on this review, a set of fields extracted from the previous analysis are proposed that could be part of a meta-annotation process to emotionally tag educational videos stored in repositories.

Keywords: Emotions · Educational videos · Meta-annotation

1 Introduction

The growing popularity of social networks, as well as the possibilities offered by mobile phones to easily create digital media resources, have generated a rapidly growing volume of media resources (images, music and videos), which has driven a great demand to manage, retrieve and understand these resources [1, 2]. This phenomenon has also reached the educational field [3, 4].

Within the range of multimedia materials, the ease for creating and publishing videos offered by web tools and social networks has turned these into resources that are used both in formal and informal education. Reference is made here to those videos that fulfill a previously formulated didactic objective [5].

Therefore, being able to manage and organize educational videos is a necessity [6]. To do so, metadata that allow system storage, recommendation, and interoperability, among others, are required.

M. J. Abásolo and G. F. Olmedo Cifuentes (Eds.): jAUTI 2021, CCIS 1597, pp. 53–69, 2022.
https://doi.org/10.1007/978-3-031-22210-8_4

Metadata is information that is created to describe digital or physical objects. According to [7], "Metadata are defined as information that describes, identifies, explains, or defines a resource for the purpose of facilitating its retrieval, use, or management." Metadata act as a guide that allows defining how to tag a resource. This guide, in most cases, includes a vocabulary. "A vocabulary is a recommended list of appropriate values to have the maximum degree of semantic interoperability and maximize the probability that other users or systems understands the metadata" [8].

From the set of metadata that can be used to tag an educational video, this article focuses on the emotions that they evoke, particularly in students, given their importance in the learning process. Emotion "is the organism's reaction to any disturbance in the perceptual environment" [9, 10] states that "emotion and learning are closely related: on the one hand, emotion is an important means for promoting learning and, on the other, the activities carried out in the learning environment have a decisive influence on the development of affect in each student; therefore, modern cognitive approaches to learning have considered emotion as one of the constructs to take into account to understand learning processes".

A previous research [11] allowed showing the effort to meta-annotate videos and educational materials, and logging user emotions, in search of improving the response of e-learning systems. It was also possible to identify several research works that focus on educational video meta-annotation, with LOM[1] and MPEG-7[2] being the standards chosen for this purpose. Likewise, when meta-annotating videos with emotions in a standardized way, the emphasis is on the use of the EmotionML language.[3] However, in that research, little evidence was found that focused on the affective meta-annotation of educational videos.

The foregoing allows accounting for a lack of specificity when emotionally meta-annotating educational videos, which motivates the present research.

Since metadata standards (for video, educational and emotional) did not offer a definitive answer, it was decided to carry out further research to answer this question: What are the elements that could be included when annotating emotional educational videos? A review of the Emotional Databases (EDBs) that store videos was carried out to identify how these repositories characterize or tag the videos hosted there.

EDBs can be defined as a repository of emotionally tagged multimedia documents. That is, a collection of images, videos and sounds related to a wide range of emotions [12]. In short, in addition to digital objects, these databases contain high-level semantic metadata and a statistical estimate of the emotion that a subject is expected to have when exposed to each multimedia document [13].

---

[1] LOM is published in the IEEE 1484.12.1 and 1484.12.3 standards. The framework defines the data model and the vocabularies used as domains. It stands out from this standard in that it allows storing educational information.

[2] MPEG-7 allows describing multimedia content, storage formats and copyrights, as well as semantic information, including emotion logging.

[3] W3C EmotionML is a markup language that allows annotating digital objects with emotional states.

This article is organized as follows: Sect. 2 describes the methodology used to select the articles that were part of the review carried out. In Sect. 3, results are detailed. Then, results are discussed in Sect. 4. Finally, the conclusions and future work are presented.

2 Methodology

This study conducts a systematic literature review. To select bibliographic material, the methodology proposed by Kitchenham et al. [14], is used, which details the following procedure: (a) define research questions, (b) outline a search strategy (where to search, which keywords to use), (c) establish inclusion and exclusion criteria, which will be applied both for initial and final selection. The article selection process would allow answering the research question: What elements are used by researchers who have created EDBs to characterize them?

2.1 Search Strategy

For the selection of EDBs, a search was carried out to identify articles dealing with aspects related to EDB creation. This search was carried out on three bibliographic databases: ACM Digital Library, IEEE Xplore and Springer. The review was carried out over the last five years (2017–2021).

A set of keywords (in English) was used for the search: emotion, dataset, database, and video. Although the words used are somewhat generic, this allowed a significant amount of BDE to be included for analysis. Note that keywords such as "education" or "learning" were initially used, but the number of papers for analysis was not enough. The search strings (expressed in the syntax of each repository) and filters used, as well as the number of results obtained, are shown in Table 1.

Table 1. Search strings, filters, and results

Database	Search string	Filter	#Paper
ACM Digital Library	[[[Abstract: emotion] AND [Abstract: dataset]] OR [[Abstract: emotion] AND [Abstract: database]]] AND [Abstract: video] AND [Publication Date: (01/01/2017 TO 12/31/2021)]	Not applicable	143
IEEE Xplore	("Abstract":emotion dataset OR "Abstract":emotion database) AND ("Abstract":video)	emotion recognition, 2017–2021	213
Springer	((emotion AND dataset) OR (emotion AND database)) AND (video)	English, Computer Science, User Interfaces and Human Computer Interaction, 2017–2021	698

(*continued*)

Table 1. (*continued*)

Database	Search string	Filter	#Paper
Total			**1054**

2.2 Inclusion and Exclusion Criteria

Once located, the articles were screened according to inclusion and exclusion criteria. The articles were evaluated by title, abstract, and, if necessary, by full text. That procedure allowed obtain a set of primary studies that was analyzed to answer each research question.

The following inclusion criteria were used:

- [CIx1]: Articles focusing on the creation of EDBs that store emotionally tagged videos and that describe or characterize the content of such databases.
- [CIx2]: Articles written in English.
- [CIx3]: Articles published between 2017–2021.

The following exclusion criteria were used:

- [CEx1]: Articles written in a language other than English.
- [CEx2]: Articles whose full text could not be accessed.
- [CEx3]: Articles in non-reviewed journals or informal literature.

2.3 Preliminary and Final Process

Out of the 1054 articles that were obtained from the search carried out, those where the title or abstract indicated the creation of an EDB were selected. Thus, 28 articles were obtained: 10 from ACM, 6 from Springer and 12 from IEEE Xplore (Fig. 1). After fully reading all of them, seven additional articles from other repositories were included, found in the bibliographic references of the articles read (snowball technique[4] [15]). These were considered of interest for this research because they dealt with creating EDBs, thus expanding the documentary base used for the identification of elements that could be used to emotionally meta-annotate educational videos. After the entire process, a total of 35 articles were selected. Two articles [16, 17] that do not fit the CIx3 criterion were included because both are of interest to our research. The first article describes a prestigious BD, which is cited by several authors addressed in this work. In the second case, the paper is a survey that refers to a significant amount of BD.

---

[4] Review of the set of references of the studies included by using the defined protocol or by expert suggestion.

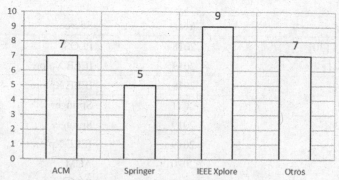

Fig. 1. Amount of selected papers sort by source

These 35 selected articles were reviewed in search of the elements used by the authors to characterize the emotional databases. Based on this first analysis, seven articles that did not allow answering the research question were excluded. Therefore, the final review was carried out over 28 articles (Table 2 and Fig. 2) to identify the elements that could meta-annotate the educational videos stored in emotional databases (see Fig. 3).

Table 2. List of articles for the final review (sort by Code).

Code	Year	Source
Abtahi18 [18]	2018	IEEE Xplore
Barros18 [19]	2018	IEEE Xplore
Baveye15 [16]	2015	IEEE Xplore
Boccignone17 [20]	2017	ACM
Conneau17 [21]	2017	IEEE Xplore
Doyran21 [22]	2021	Springer
González-Meneses19 [12]	2019	Springer
Gupta18 [23]	2018	arXiv.org
Haamer18 [24]	2018	intechopen.com
Happy17 [25]	2017	ACM
Kaixin19 [26]	2019	ACM
Kollias21 [27]	2021	arXiv.org
Kossaifi17 [28]	2017	ACM
Liliana18 [29]	2018	ACM

(continued)

Table 2. (*continued*)

Code	Year	Source
Livingstone18 [30]	2018	PLOS
Nazareth19 [31]	2019	IEEE Xplore
Nguyen19 [32]	2019	IEEE Xplore
Nonis21 [33]	2021	Springer
Sapiński19 [34]	2019	Springer
Seuss19 [35]	2019	IEEE Xplore
Shen20 [36]	2020	ACM
Soleymani17 [37]	2017	iBUG web page
Song19 [38]	2019	IEEE Xplore
Vidal20 [39]	2020	ACM
Wang15 [17]	2015	IEEE Xplore
Xiaotian20 [40]	2020	IEEE Xplore
Ya17 [41]	2017	Springer
Zhalehpour17 [42]	2017	IEEE Xplore

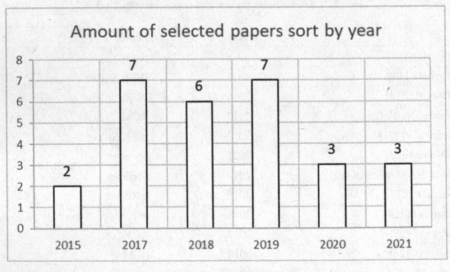

Fig. 2. Amount of selected papers sort by year

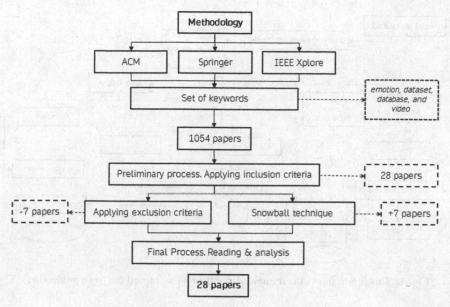

Fig. 3. Methodology summary (own production)

3 Results

This section presents the results achieved based on the review carried out over the 28 selected articles. The articles describe the creation of EDBs that store emotionally tagged videos; they also analyze related works and offer comparative tables that allow contrasting the various EDBs. In this article, this information is used as a basis to propose a set of elements that could be considered to meta-annotate educational videos published in a repository.

Figure 4 shows a diagram that summarizes the main aspects considered in the selected works. As it can be seen, the main elements that allow describing an emotionally tagged video focus mainly on how emotions are expressed, how annotations are made, and the emotional model.

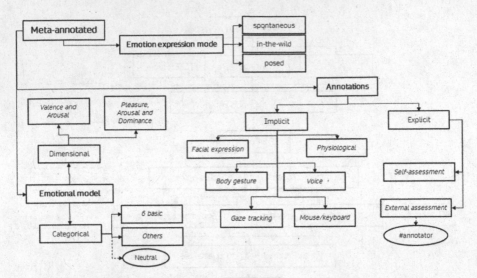

Fig. 4. This figure shows the framework for the review carried out (own production)

3.1 Emotion Expression Mode

When the authors consider the mode in which emotions are expressed when characterizing EDBs, they focus on how the video was generated. That is, what were the characteristics of the process used to obtain the emotions? The following three subcategories were obtained as a result of what was found in the articles: *posed*, *spontaneous* and *in-the-wild*. In the first case, participants (these can be actors or volunteers) are asked to show different emotional expressions. The second subcategory corresponds to emotions that are obtained from spontaneous reactions, while the third one includes emotions that are recorded in a natural context (or ecologically valid).

Most of the articles that were reviewed (17, or 60% of the total), make use of this characterization element (see Table 2). Only three of them make use of all three subcategories [12, 18, 28]. The majority (15) include *posed*, and three use this subcategory exclusively [20, 34, 42]. It is followed by the *in-the-wild* (10) and *spontaneous* (7) subcategories. Only [19] uses the *in-the-wild* subcategory only, and the *spontaneous* subcategory always appears combined with another subcategory.

3.2 Annotations

There are two ways to emotionally tag videos: implicit and explicit [37]. In the implicit method, emotional tagging is inferred from one of the automatic recognition techniques [43] (physiological, facial recognition, voice analysis, and so forth), whereas in the explicit method, the user/participant can be asked for a tag directly, using affective self-assessment forms, or using experts or scorers (quantity is important here).

More than 78% (22) of the articles reviewed here makes use of this category (Annotations) to characterize EDBs (see Table 3). In contrast, eight authors consider both subcategories to characterize EDBs, while the rest use one or the other.

Table 3. Authors that discuss emotion expression modes

Author	Posed	Spontaneous	In-the-wild
Abtahi et al. [18]	✓	✓	✓
Barros et al. [19]			✓
Boccignone et al. [20]	✓		
González-Meneses et al. [12]	✓	✓	✓
Gupta et al. [23]	✓		✓
Haamer et al. [24]	✓	✓	
Li Xiaotian et al. [40]		✓	✓
Kollias and Zafeiriou [27]	✓		✓
Kossaifi et al. [28]	✓	✓	✓
Liliana et al. [29]	✓	✓	
Livingstone and Russo [30]	✓		
Nguyen et al. [32]	✓	✓	
Sapiński et al. [34]	✓		
Seuss et al. [35]	✓		✓
Vidal et al. [39]	✓		✓
Li Ya et al. [41]	✓		✓
Zhalehpour et al. [42]	✓		

Table 4. Authors that log how EDBs implement annotations

Implicit	Explicit	Both
Abtahi et al. [18]	Happy et al. [25]	Baveye et al. [16]
Haamer et al. [24]	Kossaifi et al. [28]	Boccignone et al. [20]
Li Xiaotian et al. [40]	Livingstone and Russo [30]	Conneau et al. [21]
Liliana et al. [29]	Nguyen et al. [32]	Doyran et al. [22]
Sapiński et al. [34]	Nonis et al. [33]	Kollias and Zafeiriou [27]
Seuss et al. [35]		Nazareth et al. [31]
Song et al. [38]		Soleymani and Pantic [37]
		Wang et al. [17]

3.3 Emotional Model

For emotional scoring, two models are generally used – categorical and dimensional [44]. In the former, emotions can be described by discrete values, while in the latter, a continuous and n-dimensional space is used. The categorical model uses six basic emotions mainly: anger, disgust, fear, happiness, sadness and surprise [45], to which the "neutral" category is usually added (which indicates an initial state or neutral expression used as a starting point for the measurement). Also, depending on the intention of the research, *ad-hoc* categories can be used, such as for educational videos. If the dimensional approach is used, values are typically registered in two or three dimensions. Thus it is possible to register valence and activation (VA), or Pleasure-Arousal-Dominance (PAD) [46] (Table 5).

Table 5. Authors that use the emotional model

Categorical	Dimensional	Both
Abtahi et al. [18]	Kossaifi et al. [28]	Barros et al. [19]
González-Meneses et al. [12]	Nazareth et al. [31]	Baveye et al. [16]
Happy et al. [25]	Li Xiaotian et al. [40]	Boccignone et al. [20]
Kaixin Ma et al. [26]		Doyran et al. [22]
Liliana et al. [29]		Gupta et al. [23]
Nguyen et al. [32]		Haamer et al. [24]
Shen et al. [36]		Kollias and Zafeiriou [27]
Li Ya et al. [41]		Livingstone and Russo [30]
Zhalehpour et al. [42]		Nonis et al. [33]
		Song et al. [38]
		Wang et al. [17]

As regards this third category, there is also a high percentage (82%) of articles that uses the emotional model to characterize EDBs (see Table 4). Eleven articles use both models (categorical/dimensional) for characterization, although a preference for categorical models (20) over dimensional ones (14) is noted.

4 Discussion

The analysis carried out in this section allows identifying some of the elements that could be part of a standardized meta-annotation proposal. The section is organized based on the main categories. Also, the topic of academic emotions in educational videos is addressed. It is aimed at proposing meta-annotated elements that consider emotions in the educational context.

4.1 Emotion Expression Mode

For each emotion expression model (*posed*, *spontaneous* and *in-the-wild*) it would be desirable to have a set of elements that define the corresponding description, depending on the method used. For example, in the case of *posed* expression, indicating whether it is professional actors or volunteers who express the emotion (and possibly their age and sex) as is done in [28, 30, 34, 35]; in the case of *spontaneous* expression, indicating what was the stimulus that caused the emotion is, as done in [18, 29, 32, 40]; and in the case of *in-the-wild* expression, describing the characteristics of the environment in which the expression took place, as done in [23], or the source from where videos were extracted, as done in [27, 28, 39]. Defining these aspects that characterize each mode will require further research.

4.2 Annotations

Within the set of elements that can be used to characterize implicit annotations, it would be desirable to indicate which data collection technique(s) were used and are stored in the database with the videos. Figure 1 only shows the names used to group these techniques, but the specific techniques used should also be indicated, as in [8, 18, 36, 40].

Similarly, when explicitly using the evaluation (external scorers or affective self-evaluation) this information should be registered. Particularly, when using external annotators, the number of annotators should be indicated (see #annotators in Fig. 1). The importance of registering this value is because, on the one hand, the number of annotators can range from a few experts [22, 23] to crowdsourcing [17, 25, 37], among others; and, on the other hand, this number could account for the statistical significance and reliability of the emotion associated with the video. When it comes to affective self-assessment, the instrument or form used could be mentioned; for example, [18, 25, 40], among others, mention that Self-Assessment Manikin [47] was used. This data is relevant because it allows knowing the strengths and weaknesses associated with the instrument used to obtain the emotional tag.

4.3 Emotional Model

When characterizing the emotional model, it should be considered that, since there are different theoretical models for representing emotions, it would be desirable that most of these could be used when tagging a video. The EmotionML [48] language could be used as reference, since its vocabulary includes a significant number of such emotional models.

Most of the articles analyzed (26) do not refer to educational videos, so they do not address aspects related to the meta-annotation of this type of videos. When tagging educational videos, the emotions or the emotional model that should be used have to be taken into account. As stated by [49], defining the emotional state of a user is not a simple task, and it becomes even more complex in an educational setting.

One of the aspects that adds complexity is being able to answer the question "What are the most relevant emotions in the educational process?". Authors such as [50] answer this question by proposing hope, pride, anger, anxiety, shame, hopelessness and boredom as academic emotions for students. In [51], in contrast, the authors propose confusion, frustration, shame and pride. For [49], some of the emotions that appear in the educational context are boredom, surprise, confusion and loss of motivation. Meanwhile, [52] studied whether negative emotions such as confusion can be beneficial for learning. In the same sense, [9] finds that negative emotions or moods, such as puzzlement, frustration, confusion, uncertainty, worry or anger, could lead students to resume or redirect their learning process. In 2021, [53] introduces an affective model that measures student engagement based on their emotions and defines five levels of engagement: strong, high, medium, low, and disengaged.

In the bibliographic review, two articles were identified where learning-centered EDBs are created [12, 23]. Both use the categorical emotional model, [12] chooses to tag educational videos with emotions such as interested, boredom, frustrated, confusion, surprised, pleased, curious, happy, and neutral; while [23] uses engagement, frustration, confusion, and boredom.

It would be necessary, therefore, to take this set of emotions into account in order to characterize emotionally meta-annotated educational videos. More precisely, these emotions should be part of the controlled vocabulary of the meta-annotation proposal.

As a summary, the set of categories, subcategories and proposed vocabulary is presented in the following table (Table 6).

Table 6. Categories, subcategories, and proposed vocabulary

Category	Subcategory	Aspects to consider for vocabulary*
Emotion Expression Mode	Spontaneous	*Stimulus*
	Posed	*Professional actors, volunteers, age and sex*
	In-the-wild	Environmental characteristics, source
Annotations	Implicit	*EEG, ECG, EDA, BVP, EMG, temperature, breathing rate, action units, body posture, eye tracking, voice analysis*, and so forth
	Explicit	External: #*annotators* Self-evaluation: *SAM, FeelTrace*, etc.
Emotional Model	Categorical	6 basic/universal emotions: *anger, disgust, fear, joy, sadness and surprise* *Neutral* Other *ad-hoc* categories Using EmotionML vocabulary For educational videos: *confusion, frustration, shame, pride, enjoyment, hope, relief, anxiety, anger, boredom, hopelessness, surprise, motivation,* etc.
	Dimensional	2D: *Valence, Activation* 3D: *Pleasure, Excitement, Domination*

EEG: electroencephalogram, ECG: electrocardiogram, EDA: electrodermal activity, BVP: blood volume pulse, EMG: electromyogram, * Defining the specific vocabulary will require further research.

5 Conclusions and Future Work

In this work, 28 articles describing the creation of EDBs were reviewed. Based on this review, some descriptors of interest are proposed for the emotional meta-annotation of educational videos. This proposal includes the categories Emotion Expression Mode, Annotations, and Emotional Model, each with subcategories, and possible values that could be part of a controlled vocabulary proposal.

The proposed categories seem to appropriately characterize videos that are included in EDBs, and this information would be of interest both to the creators of EDBs and to those who use them to train emotional systems. The former could characterize the videos included in the EDBs in a standardized way, facilitating their use by researchers and promoting interoperability. The latter could make a selection from the set of videos that are best suited to train the emotional system.

It was observed that, in the specific case of educational videos, the focus is on the definition of the set of emotions that allow appropriately representing what happens in the learning process. Emotions such as confusion, frustration, shame, pride, enjoyment, hope, anxiety, anger, boredom, hopelessness, surprise, and motivation seem to have a certain level of consensus among the authors, but there is no unanimous agreement. The most widely accepted emotions among authors would have to be identified before defining a controlled vocabulary.

Therefore, further investigation is required to define the set of elements that are part of each subcategory, as well as their values. These elements should be associated with a controlled vocabulary, if possible.

Acknowledgment. This work has been partially funded by the MCIyU of Spain (Project RTI2018-096986-B-C31), the Government of Aragon (Project AffectiveLab-T60-20R), the III-LIDI – CIC, Faculty of Computer Science of the National University of La Plata (Project F11/023) and the FCEyN of the National University of La Pampa (RCD 484/20).

References

1. Zhao, S., Wang, S., Soleymani, M., Joshi, D., Ji, Q.: Affective computing for large-scale heterogeneous multimedia data: a survey. ACM Trans. Multimed. Comput. Commun. Appl. **15**, 93:1–93:32 (2019). https://doi.org/10.1145/3363560
2. Duran, D., Chanchí, G., Arciniegas, J.L., Baldassarri, S.: A semantic recommender system for iDTV based on educational competencies. In: Abásolo, M.J., Almeida, P., Pina Amargós, J. (eds.) jAUTI 2016. CCIS, vol. 689, pp. 47–61. Springer, Cham (2017). https://doi.org/10.1007/978-3-319-63321-3_4
3. Almeida, C., Almeida, P.: Online Educational Videos: how to produce them according to teenagers' preferences and teachers' approval. In: Ferraz de Abreu, J., Abásolo Guerrero, M.J., Almeida, P., and Silva, T. (eds.) Proceedings of the 9th Iberoamerican Conference on Applications and Usability of Interactive TV - jAUTI 2020, pp. 66–71. UA Editora, Aveiro, Portugal (2021). https://doi.org/10.34624/ha5s-8q59
4. Vargas-Arcila, A.M., Baldassarri, S., Herrera, J.L.A.: Marking up educational multimedia content in IPTV environments: a proposal. In: Abásolo, M.J., Kulesza, R. (eds.) jAUTI 2014. CCIS, vol. 389, pp. 35–48. Springer, Cham (2015). https://doi.org/10.1007/978-3-319-22656-9_3
5. Bravo Ramos, L.: ¿Qué es el vídeo educativo? Comunicar (1996)
6. Vargas-Arcila, A.M., Baldassarri, S., Arciniegas-Herrera, J.L.: Study and comparison of metadata schemas for the description of multimedia resources. In: Abásolo, M.J., Perales, F.J.,

Bibiloni, A. (eds.) jAUTI/CTVDI -2015. CCIS, vol. 605, pp. 59–73. Springer, Cham (2016). https://doi.org/10.1007/978-3-319-38907-3_6

7. Vargas-Arcila, A.M., Baldassarri, S., Arciniegas, J.L.: Análisis de Esquemas de Metadatos para la Marcación de Contenidos Multimedia en Televisión Digital. Inf. Tecnológica **26**, 139–154 (2015). https://doi.org/10.4067/S0718-07642015000600016

8. Deco, C., Bender, C., Saer, J.: Ponderación de metadatos de recursos educativos como forma de mejorar los resultados de una búsqueda. Energeia **IX**, 5–9 (2011)

9. Feidakis, M.: Chapter 11 - a review of emotion-aware systems for e-learning in virtual environments. In: Caballé, S., Clarisó, R. (eds.) Formative Assessment, Learning Data Analytics and Gamification, pp. 217–242. Academic Press, Boston (2016). https://doi.org/10.1016/B978-0-12-803637-2.00011-7

10. Arboleda, R., Verónica, Gallar Pérez, Y., Barrios Queipo, E.A.: Consideraciones teóricas acerca de la Computación Afectiva en el proceso de enseñanza aprendizaje de la Educación Superior. Rev. Divulg. Científica Univ. Tecnológica Indoamérica **6**, 170–175 (2017)

11. Astudillo, G.J., Sanz, C.V., Baldassarri Santalucía, S.: Revisión sistemática sobre la meta-anotación de videos educativos con emociones. Presented at the XVI Congreso de Tecnología en Educación & Educación en Tecnología - TE&ET 2021 (La Plata, 10 y 11 de junio de 2021) (2021)

12. González-Meneses, Y.N., Guerrero-García, J., Reyes-García, C.A., Olmos-Pineda, I., González-Calleros, J.M.: Formal protocol for the creation of a database of physiological and behavioral signals for the automatic recognition of emotions. In: Ruiz, P.H., Agredo-Delgado, V. (eds.) HCI-COLLAB 2019. CCIS, vol. 1114, pp. 211–226. Springer, Cham (2019). https://doi.org/10.1007/978-3-030-37386-3_16

13. Horvat, M.: A brief overview of affective multimedia databases - ProQuest. Presented at the Central European Conference on Information and Intelligent Systems, Varaždin, Croacia (2017)

14. Kitchenham, B., Brereton, O.P., Budgen, D., Turner, M., Bailey, J., Linkman, S.: Systematic literature reviews in software engineering – a systematic literature review. Inf. Softw. Technol. **51**, 7–15 (2009). https://doi.org/10.1016/j.infsof.2008.09.009

15. Greenhalgh, T., Peacock, R.: Effectiveness and efficiency of search methods in systematic reviews of complex evidence: audit of primary sources. BMJ **331**, 1064–1065 (2005). https://doi.org/10.1136/bmj.38636.593461.68

16. Baveye, Y., Dellandréa, E., Chamaret, C., Chen, L.: LIRIS-ACCEDE: a video database for affective content analysis. IEEE Trans. Affect. Comput. **6**, 43–55 (2015). https://doi.org/10.1109/TAFFC.2015.2396531

17. Wang, S., Ji, Q.: Video affective content analysis: a survey of state-of-the-art methods. IEEE Trans. Affect. Comput. **6**, 410–430 (2015). https://doi.org/10.1109/TAFFC.2015.2432791

18. Abtahi, F., Ro, T., Li, W., Zhu, Z.: Emotion analysis using audio/video, EMG and EEG: a dataset and comparison study. In: 2018 IEEE Winter Conference on Applications of Computer Vision (WACV), pp. 10–19 (2018). https://doi.org/10.1109/WACV.2018.00008

19. Barros, P., Churamani, N., Lakomkin, E., Siqueira, H., Sutherland, A., Wermter, S.: The OMG-emotion behavior dataset. In: 2018 International Joint Conference on Neural Networks (IJCNN), pp. 1–7 (2018). https://doi.org/10.1109/IJCNN.2018.8489099

20. Boccignone, G., Conte, D., Cuculo, V., Lanzarotti, R.: AMHUSE: a multimodal dataset for HUmour SEnsing. In: Proceedings of the 19th ACM International Conference on Multimodal Interaction, pp. 438–445. Association for Computing Machinery, New York (2017). https://doi.org/10.1145/3136755.3136806

21. Conneau, A.-C., Hajlaoui, A., Chetouani, M., Essid, S.: EMOEEG: a new multimodal dataset for dynamic EEG-based emotion recognition with audiovisual elicitation. In: 2017 25th European Signal Processing Conference (EUSIPCO), pp. 738–742 (2017). https://doi.org/10.23919/EUSIPCO.2017.8081305

22. Doyran, M., et al.: MUMBAI: multi-person, multimodal board game affect and interaction analysis dataset. J. Multimodal User Interfaces **15**(4), 373–391 (2021). https://doi.org/10. 1007/s12193-021-00364-0
23. Gupta, A., D'Cunha, A., Awasthi, K., Balasubramanian, V.: DAiSEE: towards user engagement recognition in the wild. arXiv:160901885 Cs (2018)
24. Haamer, R.E., Rusadze, E., Lüsi, I., Ahmed, T., Escalera, S., Anbarjafari, G.: Chapter 3. Review on emotion recognition databases. In: Human-Robot Interaction: Theory and Application, pp. 40–63. BoD – Books on Demand (2018)
25. Happy, S.L., Patnaik, P., Routray, A., Guha, R.: The Indian spontaneous expression database for emotion recognition. IEEE Trans. Affect. Comput. **8**, 131–142 (2017). https://doi.org/10. 1109/TAFFC.2015.2498174
26. Ma, K., Wang, X., Yang, X., Zhang, M., Girard, J.M., Morency, L.-P.: ElderReact: a multimodal dataset for recognizing emotional response in aging adults. In: 2019 International Conference on Multimodal Interaction, pp. 349–357. Association for Computing Machinery, New York (2019). https://doi.org/10.1145/3340555.3353747
27. Kollias, D., Zafeiriou, S.: Affect analysis in-the-wild: valence-arousal, expressions, action units and a unified framework. arXiv:210315792 Cs. (2021)
28. Kossaifi, J., Tzimiropoulos, G., Todorovic, S., Pantic, M.: AFEW-VA database for valence and arousal estimation in-the-wild. Image Vis. Comput. **65**, 23–36 (2017). https://doi.org/10. 1016/j.imavis.2017.02.001
29. Liliana, D.Y., Basaruddin, T., Oriza, I.I.D.: The Indonesian Mixed Emotion Dataset (IMED): a facial expression dataset for mixed emotion recognition. In: Proceedings of the 2018 International Conference on Artificial Intelligence and Virtual Reality, pp. 56–60. Association for Computing Machinery, New York (2018). https://doi.org/10.1145/3293663.3293671
30. Livingstone, S.R., Russo, F.A.: The Ryerson Audio-Visual Database of Emotional Speech and Song (RAVDESS): a dynamic, multimodal set of facial and vocal expressions in North American English. PLoS ONE **13**, e0196391 (2018). https://doi.org/10.1371/journal.pone. 0196391
31. Nazareth, D.S., Jansen, M.-P., Truong, K.P., Westerhof, G.J., Heylen, D.: MEMOA: introducing the multi-modal emotional memories of older adults database. In: 2019 8th International Conference on Affective Computing and Intelligent Interaction (ACII), pp. 697–703 (2019). https://doi.org/10.1109/ACII.2019.8925462
32. Nguyen, K., Ghinita, G., Naveed, M., Shahabi, C.: A privacy-preserving, accountable and spam-resilient geo-marketplace. In: Proceedings of the 27th ACM SIGSPATIAL International Conference on Advances in Geographic Information Systems, pp. 299–308. Association for Computing Machinery, New York (2019). https://doi.org/10.1145/3347146.3359072
33. Nonis, F., et al.: Building an ecologically valid facial expression database – behind the scenes. In: Antona, M., Stephanidis, C. (eds.) HCII 2021. LNCS, vol. 12768, pp. 599–616. Springer, Cham (2021). https://doi.org/10.1007/978-3-030-78092-0_42
34. Sapiński, T., Kamińska, D., Pelikant, A., Ozcinar, C., Avots, E., Anbarjafari, G.: Multimodal database of emotional speech, video and gestures. In: Zhang, Z., Suter, D., Tian, Y., Branzan Albu, A., Sidère, N., Jair Escalante, H. (eds.) ICPR 2018. LNCS, vol. 11188, pp. 153–163. Springer, Cham (2019). https://doi.org/10.1007/978-3-030-05792-3_15
35. Seuss, D., et al.: Emotion expression from different angles: a video database for facial expressions of actors shot by a camera array. In: 2019 8th International Conference on Affective Computing and Intelligent Interaction (ACII), pp. 35–41 (2019). https://doi.org/10.1109/ ACII.2019.8925458
36. Shen, G., Wang, X., Duan, X., Li, H., Zhu, W.: MEmoR: a dataset for multimodal emotion reasoning in videos. In: Proceedings of the 28th ACM International Conference on Multimedia, pp. 493–502. Association for Computing Machinery, New York (2020). https://doi.org/ 10.1145/3394171.3413909

37. Soleymani, M., Pantic, M.: Multimedia implicit tagging. In: Burgoon, J.K., Magnenat-Thalmann, N., Pantic, M., Vinciarelli, A. (eds.) Social Signal Processing, pp. 369–376. Cambridge University Press, United Kingdom (2017)
38. Song, T., Zheng, W., Lu, C., Zong, Y., Zhang, X., Cui, Z.: MPED: a multi-modal physiological emotion database for discrete emotion recognition. IEEE Access **7**, 12177–12191 (2019). https://doi.org/10.1109/ACCESS.2019.2891579
39. Vidal, A., Salman, A., Lin, W.-C., Busso, C.: MSP-face corpus: a natural audiovisual emotional database. In: Proceedings of the 2020 International Conference on Multimodal Interaction, pp. 397–405. Association for Computing Machinery, New York (2020). https://doi.org/10.1145/3382507.3418872
40. Li, X., Zhang, X., Yang, H., Duan, W., Dai, W., Yin, L.: An EEG-based multi-modal emotion database with both posed and authentic facial actions for emotion analysis. In: 2020 15th IEEE International Conference on Automatic Face and Gesture Recognition (FG 2020), pp. 336–343 (2020). https://doi.org/10.1109/FG47880.2020.00050
41. Li, Y., Tao, J., Chao, L., Bao, W., Liu, Y.: CHEAVD: a Chinese natural emotional audio–visual database. J. Ambient. Intell. Humaniz. Comput. **8**(6), 913–924 (2016). https://doi.org/10.1007/s12652-016-0406-z
42. Zhalehpour, S., Onder, O., Akhtar, Z., Erdem, C.E.: BAUM-1: a spontaneous audio-visual face database of affective and mental states. IEEE Trans. Affect. Comput. **8**, 300–313 (2017). https://doi.org/10.1109/TAFFC.2016.2553038
43. Picard, R.W.: Affective computing for HCI. In: Proceedings of HCI International (the 8th International Conference on Human-Computer Interaction) on Human-Computer Interaction: Ergonomics and User Interfaces-Volume I - Volume I, pp. 829–833. L. Erlbaum Associates Inc., Hillsdale (1999)
44. Gunes, H., Schuller, B.: Categorical and dimensional affect analysis in continuous input: current trends and future directions. Image Vis. Comput. **31**, 120–136 (2013). https://doi.org/10.1016/j.imavis.2012.06.016
45. Ekman, P.: Basic emotions. In: Dalgleish, T., Power, M. (eds.) Handbook of Cognition and Emotion, pp. 45–60. Wiley, Hoboken (1999)
46. Bakker, I., van der Voordt, T., Vink, P., de Boon, J.: Pleasure, Arousal, Dominance: Mehrabian and Russell revisited. Curr. Psychol. **33**(3), 405–421 (2014). https://doi.org/10.1007/s12144-014-9219-4
47. Bradley, M.M., Lang, P.J.: Measuring emotion: the self-assessment manikin and the semantic differential. J. Behav. Ther. Exp. Psychiatry **25**, 49–59 (1994). https://doi.org/10.1016/0005-7916(94)90063-9
48. Baggia, P., Pelachaud, C., Peter, C., Zovato, E.: Emotion Markup Language (EmotionML) 1.0 (2014). https://www.w3.org/TR/emotionml/
49. Santos, O.C., Saneiro, M., Salmeron-Majadas, S., Boticario, J.G.: A methodological approach to eliciting affective educational recommendations. In: 2014 IEEE 14th International Conference on Advanced Learning Technologies, pp. 529–533 (2014). https://doi.org/10.1109/ICALT.2014.234
50. Pekrun, R., Goetz, T., Titz, W., Perry, R.P.: Academic emotions in students' self-regulated learning and achievement: a program of qualitative and quantitative research. Educ. Psychol. **37**, 91–105 (2002). https://doi.org/10.1207/S15326985EP3702_4
51. Immordino-Yang, M.H., Damasio, A.: We feel, therefore we learn: the relevance of affective and social neuroscience to education. Mind Brain Educ. **1**, 3 (2007). https://doi.org/10.1111/j.1751-228X.2007.00004.x

52. D'Mello, S., Lehman, B., Pekrun, R., Graesser, A.: Confusion can be beneficial for learning. Learn. Instr. **29**, 153–170 (2014). https://doi.org/10.1016/j.learninstruc.2012.05.003
53. Altuwairqi, K., Jarraya, S.K., Allinjawi, A., Hammami, M.: A new emotion–based affective model to detect student's engagement. J. King Saud Univ. - Comput. Inf. Sci. **33**, 99–109 (2021). https://doi.org/10.1016/j.jksuci.2018.12.008

Active and Healthy Aging: The Role of a Proactive Information Assistant Embedded on TV

Gabriel Faria(✉) ⓘ, Telmo Silva(✉) ⓘ, and Jorge Abreu(✉) ⓘ

DigiMedia, Department of Communication and Art, University of Aveiro, Aveiro, Portugal
{g.martinsfaria,tsilva,jfa}@ua.pt

Abstract. Population ageing has become a general issue due to technological and scientific progress that has increased citizens' life expectancy. Because of this, it is essential to develop strategies to promote senior people's physical and mental well-being. Local events (such as popular festivals in the residential area and other types of gatherings), which allow seniors to interact with other people socially, are a potential contribution to improving their quality of life. The dissemination of those events is, therefore, essential. Furthermore, to ensure that older people have a good quality of life, it is inevitable to provide them with tools that allow them to frequently self-monitor their health and medication intake status easily since it is in the third have that we observe a more considerable prevalence of physical and cognitive diseases. However, transmitting this information to older adults, who may have limitations in digital skills, requires efficient approaches. Since the television is widely used among seniors, it may be an adequate device for implementing an advanced information system integrated with a customisable proactive personal assistant like the ProSeniorTV system addressed in this paper. This article presents the results generated by a focus group session with the collaboration of 6 older adults to evaluate a set of usage scenarios idealised for ProSeniorTV. The feedback from the focus group participants showed that such a system would be beneficial in promoting seniors' participation in social activities held in their area of residence and helping them remember to take their medication.

Keywords: Health monitoring · Interactive television · Local community · Medication intake monitoring · Personal information assistant · Proactivity and senior population

1 Introduction

The improvement of the population's living conditions allied to technological development has led to the growth of the number of older people [1]. Globally it is expected that by 2050 the elderly population will double [2].

© Springer Nature Switzerland AG 2022
M. J. Abásolo and G. F. Olmedo Cifuentes (Eds.): jAUTI 2021, CCIS 1597, pp. 70–84, 2022.
https://doi.org/10.1007/978-3-031-22210-8_5

In Portugal, according to INE [3], the current value of 159 older adults per 100 young people is also expected to double by 2080. These data reveal that, gradually, there will be a greater need to create and adopt strategies aimed at the well-being of the elderly [1, 2].

By participating in regular activities that trigger social interactions, seniors can develop the feeling of belonging to the community where they live, an essential factor that promotes healthy ageing [1, 4]. Thus, this age group needs access to information media that inform them about social activities (promoting interactions with other people) that can be autonomously used by them [5]. The same authors [5] refer that television (TV) may be usefully employed for this purpose since it is a medium highly used by seniors. For that reason, integrating new technologies in such a medium may reduce the reluctance of this age group to adopt them.

According to Silva [1], the elderly's characteristics justify that information must be proactively provided to them without requiring a research process by the seniors. Hence, a personal assistant (an automated software that helps human users through natural language [6]) integrated on TV and able to act proactively could be decisive in allowing senior people to benefit from local and personalised information. This will help people play a more active role within their community, resulting in greater levels of social engagement and life quality. The examples exposed by Silva [1] and Abreu [7] justify the relevance of this perspective. In the first case [1], interactive television (iTV) proved to be an effective way to present information about public and social services to seniors. The second case [7] proved to be a good promoter of seniors' social interactions and health care.

It is also important to mention that, in this sense, the creation of smartphones embedded with gradually more sophisticated sensors and the design of new technological devices, such as smartwatches that also have sensors to monitor the vital signs of their users, further enhances the character of the TV as a robust health care device. That happens due to the emergence of iTV, once it becomes possible to integrate these devices into TV apps by creating multi-device systems in which the TV is the central element [8].

Structurally, in the second section of this article, a description of senior people is made, namely, their physical, cognitive and social characteristics. The third section presents the proposal of an informative personal assistant for TV (*ProSeniorTV*), intending to promote the quality of life of the elderly.

In Sect. 4, we present the methodology adopted for this study, which was based on a focus group session with the collaboration of senior citizens. This focus group evaluated a set of usage scenarios idealised for the TV assistant. Section 5 presents the results/discussion regarding the focus group.

Next, the sixth section reflects on the issue of adopting strategies that allow seniors to integrate into society actively and resumes the results of the focus group session. Finally, in the seventh section, we present the work we want to focus on in the future.

2   Seniors

As mentioned above, we currently witness a generalised ageing process in the population
[1]. Combined with the specificities of senior citizens (in physical, cognitive, and social
terms), this ageing process intensifies the concern about the well-being of this age group
[1, 2].

According to Boldy [9], most seniors prefer to live in their homes for as long as
possible rather than under the care of professionals. Unconsciously, this decision may
place seniors in an environment of loneliness [10] since they are generally disadvantaged
because they do not know how to access public services and social activities [1]. This
arises due to the high levels of info exclusion and technological illiteracy that are typical
among the majority of the elderly [5, 11]. However, this generalised ageing process
ends up giving rise to a paradigm shift where, gradually, the elderly seek to spend their
time in the company of family and friends [12]. Consequently, this paradigm shift is
a turning point in the fight against loneliness among the elderly since, according to
[10], promoting social contacts is a fundamental factor in preventing loneliness. At the
same time, and despite the paradigm shift mentioned above, the ageing process causes
biological changes in physical and cognitive terms. Physically, seniors are more affected
by a higher prevalence of disabilities and diseases when compared to younger age groups
[13]. Cognitively, as people age, they lose capacities. For example, it becomes harder to
recover short-term memories and to direct their attention to specific tasks [13, 14].

Even though the elderly's biological characteristics represent a significant obstacle
to adopting an active and healthy ageing process, these characteristics can be overcome.
According to [15] and [16], involvement in outdoor activities is related to better mental
health and quality of life among seniors. Participating in social contexts also results
in beneficial effects, specifically regarding seniors' mental health [17]. That happens
because by feeling socially engaged in their community, seniors can experience an active
and healthy ageing process [18].

As shown, the elderly tend to socially isolate themselves [10], which degrades their
quality of life. Therefore, it is essential to implement measures to promote active and
healthy ageing.

At the same time, given the potentialities of new technologies, it is now possible
to implement ambient assisted living (AAL) contexts in which the safety and security
of seniors are highly increased [19]. According to the same authors [19], this context
allows older adults to use technologies that improve self-longevity, for example, by
using personal assistants (PAs) to remember medication intake through natural language
notifications. As mentioned above, since older adults have a more significant probability
of developing physical and cognitive diseases requiring regular medication intake, using
such technologies may be a valuable resource for the daily life of this age group.

3   Proposal for a Proactive Personal Information Assistant
for Television

This article describes a potential solution that may be at the origin of creating a context
in which the elderly can autonomously access relevant information and notifications to

remain active and healthy during their lifetime. As Buccoliero and Bellio [20] mentioned, nowadays' seniors were not born in the digital age, so they struggle to adapt to emerging technologies. These difficulties are exponentially increased if we consider their physical and cognitive characteristics [11, 12], which often affect their daily lives (including the interaction with technologies). Information and Communication Technologies have great potential to disseminate activities that promote healthy ageing and a better quality of life. Also, nowadays' technologies can even monitor users' vital signs and notify them when it detects body malfunctions which may be very useful for the quality of life of older adults. However, it must be recognised that they must be adapted to the elderly, given that most current technological solutions are developed for a young audience [5].

Typically, seniors prefer access to information without the need to research it [1], so the proactive nature of most PAs [18] may transform these assistants into essential tools for adapting technology to seniors. Furthermore, proactive PAs can anticipate the needs of seniors, directing them to adequate, personalised, and valuable information [21].

Television (TV), a medium that allows simple access to information [22], is a technological device widely adopted in family contexts, which highlights the societal importance of this medium [23]. Technological developments have also allowed the transformation of TV into an interactive medium, making it possible to: i) interact with TV content [24]; ii) have access to content from several sources [25]; and iii) access new features beyond the typical content visualisation (e.g., telecare services) [26]. It is also important to mention that TV is a technology largely present in the daily lives of Portuguese seniors, who spend more than 21 h a week watching TV [27]. Moreover, most of the senior population has access to leisure activities through TV (e.g., watching movies, soap operas, and live-streamed parties) [1].

Considering the great familiarity between seniors and TV, the potential of PAs and the scant work carried out in this area, we propose the creation of an informative personal assistant for the TV. The aim is to create an assistant that must be able to direct seniors to personalised information about local events and about their vital signs monitorisation (e.g., heart rate) through the TV. By implementing this solution, information about events such as popular parties at the user's area of residence and other types of gatherings will then be transmitted to the elderly to enhance their participation in those events. Factors such as involvement in the local community and regular social interactions are fundamental to promoting active ageing [8, 26]. Therefore, we think it makes sense to focus on the dissemination/suggestion of events promoted by the seniors' local community because we believe it is this kind of event that presents the most significant potential for the promotion of an active ageing process.

Furthermore, the highest levels of prevalence of diseases among the elderly require higher care to preserve these citizens' quality of life [13]. In this regard, if the proposed PA detects that the elder's vital signs are altered, which might indicate, for example, that he forgot to take his regular medication, then the assistant must question the user on whether he has taken his medication or not. Thus, the proactivity of the PA to read and interpret these vital signs variations will help avoid possible severe consequences on the health of the elder user.

It is intended that the proposed solution (named *ProSeniorTV* and represented in Fig. 1) must work as an aggregator of information regarding the dissemination of events promoted by local organisations, such as Municipal Councils, Parish Councils, or voluntary organisations. After collecting information about the events (date, time, place, and typology) by consulting local organisations' websites or local newspapers, the solution will then present the results through TV in the form of notifications to seniors. These notifications will show the descriptive text of the event and the corresponding narration of it (to ease the interpretation). The user will be questioned about their interest in participating in the event and will have the opportunity to confirm their participation using the keys on the remote control. The system must be capable of notifying the user whenever it verifies the existence of a new event and shall do it in opportune moments that do not affect the content viewing experience, such as when turning on the TV, during advertising viewing, or when zapping.

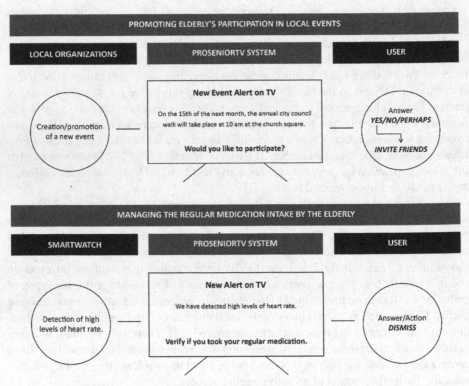

Fig. 1. Representation of the working process of the *ProSeniorTV* system.

For example, when the City Council of the senior's area of residence publishes a new event on its website, the *ProSeniorTV* system will automatically collect the event information and notify the user through the TV, asking him about his interest in participating. The user will be able to respond with – yes, no, and perhaps. When the user's answer is 'perhaps', then the system will re-notify him in the future to ensure whether he wants to participate in a specific event. When the user confirms participation, the system will regularly remind him about the event, ensuring he does not forget it.

Still, considering the user's choices about the events referred being the ones he has an interest in, the ProSeniorTV assistant will suggest the invitation of his friends for those events through the TV. We hope that with this feature, seniors can share more with each other, thus, giving them a sense of being part of a community and feeling integrated into society.

Following the same logic and also as it is represented in Fig. 1, concerning the monitorisation of regular medication intake by the elderly, we want the system to analyse information collected through the user's smartwatch, namely his heart rate or other relevant data that might indicate that the senior did not take his daily medication. Hence, if it is detected, for example, that the user's heart rate is very high and knowing previously that the user takes, regularly, medication to control his blood pressure, then the ProSeniorTV assistant will present the senior with a notification through the TV, informing him about his heart rate and question the user on whether he has taken his medication or not.

4 Methodology

The primary purpose of this paper is to understand whether or not senior audiences perceive a set of usage scenarios for the *ProSeniorTV* service as applicable. Two specific scenarios were studied. In the first scenario, the service informs the user of the occurrence of a particular event and allows him to confirm his participation through an iTV system. In the second scenario, given the events the user is subscribed to, the service enables the user to invite/suggest those events to family and friends through the iTV system. These usage scenarios are outlined in Fig. 2.

As observed through the figure, the first scenario is represented by an agenda icon since it notifies the user of a specific event to be held at a certain date and time. The second scenario is represented by a friends icon since, in this case, it highlights the fact that the user has the possibility of sharing a specific event with other people.

Considering the objective mentioned above, students from the Universidade Sénior de Cacia (USIDEC), located in the district of Aveiro, were invited to participate in a focus group session. This session was crucial for this study because it allowed us to understand the senior public's opinion about the *ProSeniorTV* service through the presentation and discussion of the usage scenarios. This way, it will be easier to elaborate a list of functional requirements for the service, considering the received seniors' feedback.

It is also important to mention that to meet the concern of having a focus group session that would be as fruitful as possible, the research team previously created three videos[1] to represent each of the usage scenarios. The videos have a narration with simple language so that it was easy for the senior participants to understand what was being presented. As shown in Fig. 3, each participant answered a short characterisation questionnaire at the beginning of the session. Then the usage scenarios of the *ProSeniorTV* service were presented (using the videos) and discussed.

---

[1] https://youtube.com/playlist?list=PLEXdi7Vbvn7IEXHZ37-wsu7u0tqPqcaWT.

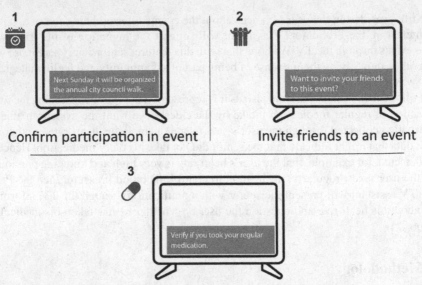

Fig. 2. Features presented during the focus group session.

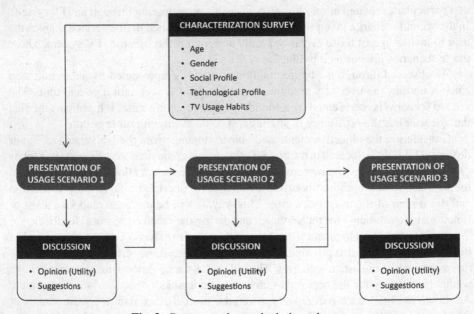

Fig. 3. Representative study design scheme.

The focus group session comprised six ($n = 6$) USIDEC students. It took place in March 2022, at the UX Lab of the Social iTV group (http://socialitv.web.ua.pt) of the University of Aveiro, for approximately 90 min. As seen in Fig. 4, this session was purposely held in this UX evaluation laboratory since it faithfully simulates a typical living room environment.

Fig. 4. Focus group session photo.

5 Results and Discussion

Two of the six individuals who participated in this study were male ($n = 33.3\%$), and the remaining 4 were female ($n = 66.7\%$). The age of the participants ranged from 64 to 80 years old and corresponded to a mean age of 74 years and a median of 75 years. As expected, all participants used TV assiduously to access, among others, informational, sports, and entertainment content. In addition, all users owned a smartphone, a tablet, or a computer and were used to using these devices to make video or voice calls, send messages, or search for information. Considering this scenario, it can be regarded that the members of this sample were already quite well acquainted with new technologies. However, the participants said they are closely related to other seniors less digitally literate and that they know their limitations regarding access to information. For that reason, the opinions presented by the participants represent a holistic view. It also should be noted that they are socially busy individuals since they reported attending several cultural and sports activities. They emphasised the activities organised by the Senior University to which they belonged.

Most participants did not suffer from serious health problems. However, P3 reported hearing difficulties, P5 mentioned that their vision problems affected the viewing of television contents, namely the reading of subtitles, and P2 and P3 showed some difficulties moving around. P4 said that he needs to take daily medication due to health problems.

When faced with the first usage scenario, where the user is notified through the TV about a specific event and can confirm their participation through the same device, all people found this feature quite interesting (P1 - "To alert people, I think it's good. I think it's a good idea"; P4 - "(…) this is interesting!").

Throughout the discussion, it was easily understood that one of the reasons for the participants to be interested in a feature of this kind results from the fact that the dissemination of events/activities held in the participants' area of residence (Aveiro) does not reach this audience or is not done in a very efficient way by local organisations. P2 refers, for example, that many times he only gets to know about the activities organised in his city after they have taken place, so he considers that in his town, a feature of this kind would be very welcome (P2 - "I think that for Aveiro it would be fascinating because they publish things after they have already happened. In Aveiro it would be essential"). P5 corroborates this idea by stating that he goes to several events with very little or no affluence and considers that most people don't know about these events due to a lack of advertisement. Moreover, P5 even mentions that the registration period for certain events extends beyond the date of the event itself, which in his opinion, misleads people (P5 - "(…) registrations open until the 9th, for example, and it (the event) was already on the 7th").

The usefulness perceived by the focus group participants regarding the first usage scenario also derives from the fact that they use TV quite assiduously (P2 - "If this (the events) are advertised like this, it reaches a lot more people"; P1 - "Yes, yes, because TV is everywhere"; P4 - "Exactly, so everyone sees it"). For this reason, the possibility of confirming participation in a particular event through TV was also well received.

The fact that some people have mobility impairments that prevent them from walking down the street and reading the billboards that local organisations typically use to disseminate their events also raised interest in this scenario (P2 - "(…) because we no longer walk down the street looking at advertisements."). In this context, P5 also mentions that the events are often publicised through the local newspaper. However, he notes that although it is a paid medium of information, it does not transmit many details about the events in his residence.

Regarding suggestions, several participants mentioned that frequent times the events are postponed or cancelled. Still, this information is not disclosed, which ends up affecting several people (P5 - "Many times the city councils publish the information about the events and people go to the places to attend the event, but then when they get to the place, that particular activity was cancelled, and nobody told anyone"). In this sense, participants suggested that the service should be able to notify about the realisation of a particular activity and its possible postponement or cancellation.

When asked about the usefulness of the second usage scenario, in which the users can invite their friends/family to a specific event in which they are registered, through the TV, the participants were also interested and thought that it would be helpful (P2 - "Yes, yes, I agree"; P4 - "(…) one is not together every day so that one could invite family and friends"; P1 - "(…) to invite to a walk, for example, it would be good").

Still, in this scenario, regarding the interaction model with the service, some people admitted that depending on the person, it might be easier to invite other people using voice commands instead of using the remote control (P2 - "You could use one or the other, right?! By voice you could invite more people"; P1 - "Maybe it's easier by voice").

Participants showed that if they received an invitation of this kind from their friends/family, they would possibly be more interested in participating in a given event (P2 - "For USIDEC activities, for example, this feature would be great, because this way, people already knew who was going to participate and would then be more interested in participating"). Therefore, they considered this an exciting way to know about the events held in their area of residence.

In general terms, all participants attributed a substantial degree of usefulness to the two proposed usage scenarios (P2 - "Useful (…)"; P1 - "It's useful and pleasant"; P5 - "(…) everything you are presenting is useful, a public utility"). This is because the presented usage scenarios seem to be closely related to the needs and characteristics of this kind of public.

In the last stage of the focus group, the participants were confronted by a third and last usage scenario, in which the iTV system was integrated with the collected information through the smartwatch of the user, namely information about their vital signs (for example, blood pressure and heart rate), notifies the user on this exact data. Specifically, in this scenario, the system detects when the user's heart rate is accelerated, possibly indicating a non-intake of the meds. Therefore, the system alerts the user of that eventuality through the TV.

Unanimously the focus group participants considered that this scenario would be very beneficial to them (P1 – Very important this scenario! Very very important"; P3 – "(…) I also think it is something useful"; P6 – "I think it's something good and I believe it will be important"). By discussing with the focus group participants, we understood that, firstly, the high interest in this type of scenario resulted from the fact that most participants needed to take daily medication. For that reason, they regularly monitor their daily medication intake (P6 – "Everyone here already needs to take drugs. Because of this, I believe that this functionality is essential"). Furthermore, the participants considered that this type of functionality might be even more relevant in cases where people need to take a significant quantity of daily medication (P1 – "(…) often, people need to take more than one pill a day, making it harder to remember to take the regular medication accurately."). P2 even referred that in a specific period of his life, he had to take medication twice a day (in the morning and at night) and considered that at the time, it was not easy remembering to take night medication. In the case of P4, he mentioned that he takes 18 pills a day (P4 – "(…) today I already took 9 pills, and later I need to take the same amount"). Considering this, P4 revealed that in his daily routine, it is essential to use reminder alarms to prevent him from forgetting to take his regular medication (P4 – "I, for example, have a reminder on my smartwatch and smartphone at 22h30 to remind me to take my medication. It is a specific pill, the most dangerous of them all, the chemotherapy pill. Otherwise, I would often forget to take it"). As a result of his experience in the nursing field, P2 reaffirms that it is common for people who need to take several types of medication to get confused and intake the wrong drugs at inappropriate moments (P2 – "(…) people who take several medications sometimes get confused. For example, they have to take pills for their blood pressure (…), and they take another kind of pill, and then their blood pressure abruptly goes down because they didn't take the proper medication. (…) this happens more often than you might think"). P2 then places great value on this type of scenario.

Secondly, the strong interest shown by the participants in this scenario is mainly since they consider that with age, it becomes more difficult to memorise information, so they think this could be an excellent way to prevent seniors from forgetting to take their regular medication, which could result in severe consequences to their health (P2 – "(…) with our age, people already start to forget to take their medication, and so it is a suitable warning"; P3 – "This is an essential scenario for the ones (…) who forget their commitments").

At this point, the participants were also aware that they would have to wear a smart-watch to access this functionality, so they were asked if this would be a problem. As mentioned earlier, all the participants were already familiar with using new technologies, so they said this would not be a problem.

In the end, although they consider this scenario quite useful and (P1 AND P2) agree that this type of notification results from a specific context in which the information provided by the smartwatch may indicate that the user has not taken his medication, P5 mentioned that the simple fact of asking the user about taking his drug is something that can have perverse effects (P5 - "I may have already taken the medication and not remember, and because they are asking me, I may be misled and take the same medication twice. I think this functionality needs some adjustments"). P6 agreed that some adjustments might be needed, but he was very interested and considered this feature very important. To prevent the elderly from taking the same medication twice, P2 then suggested that this type of scenario should be complemented with the efficient use of pill boxes that allow users, in case of doubt, to confirm whether or not they have taken their medication (P2 – "(…) by combining these means (pillboxes), in which the person places the specific medicine they have to take in each phase of the day, this type of alert prevents the elderly from taking the same medication twice. This way, the system alerts, and the person can go to the pillbox to check whether or not they have taken their medication.").

Considering that, for this study to be carried out, we relied heavily on the collaboration of the senior participants, the most critical limitation occurred during the recruiting phase. Although the sample studied was composed of only six individuals, reaching this number was challenging. This was only possible with the help of USIDEC, an institution we would like to thank in advance.

6   Final Remarks

The need to ensure that the elderly can age with quality of life has given rise to numerous research projects. Examples include projects such as + *TV4E* [1] and *iNeighbour TV* [7], which seek to respond to this through technologies.

It is also through these examples that we understood that the solution for something as complex as ensuring the active ageing of populations could be born from a hybrid perspective, in this case, by creating synergies between means of communication that have existed for a long time (e.g., TV) and new technologies (such as PAs).

Assuming that the elderly do not have high digital literacy and represent an age group highly familiarised with TV, it makes sense to create proactive assistance solutions for the elderly and integrate them into TV. As a result, it will be possible to ensure the well-being of senior people through a technological solution that is not strange to the elderly (since it will be integrated into TV) to bypass seniors' limitations.

Since these assistance solutions seek to guarantee an active ageing process, they should promote participation in activities that promote regular social interactions to involve seniors in their community. Following this perspective, this article suggests creating a proactive personal information assistant for TV whose primary goal is to help senior people.

In this sense, a focus group session was held with the collaboration of 6 students from a senior university to understand whether or not it makes sense for the elderly to have an assistant of this kind integrated into an iTV system, to inform them of the events that take place in their area of residence and about the eventuality of them had forgotten to take their regular medication.

More specifically, three usage scenarios were tested. The first one is in which the user is notified about an event through the TV, having the possibility to confirm his participation using the same device (the TV). In the second usage scenario, the user can invite friends/family to participate in the events he had previously registered for. In this case, the invitations would also be made through the TV. In the third scenario, the system notifies the user, through TV, of the eventuality that they had forgotten to take their meds, avoiding more severe consequences.

Through the focus group session, it was understood that the sample of participants used television and new technologies assiduously and that they had a regular need to participate in social activities. In this sense, their assessment of the usage scenarios we aimed to test showed that the events/activities in their residence area are often poorly advertised. The participants then highlighted that it is recurrent that they do not know about these events or activities on time, so they cannot integrate them. Faced with this frustration, the focus group participants mentioned that a system like *ProSeniorTV* would be beneficial for their daily lives, as they would have easier access to local information and because they are already very familiar with the use of TV, they mentioned that the interaction with this type of service would be easy for them, facilitating the process of registration for events/activities.

It is also important to highlight that, according to the participants, certain events are often postponed or cancelled. Often this postponement/cancellation information does not reach the elderly, which causes them to go several times to certain events on incorrect dates. In this sense, several participants suggested that, besides the *ProSeniorTV* service being able to notify the user when an event is organised, it should also inform the user when an event is postponed or cancelled.

As to the alerts presented on the TV regarding the medication intake, each participant has considered it very useful since each of them takes medication daily.

Accordingly, to the participants, the utility of this type of scenario dues to the fact that many seniors take a high quantity of medication daily, which makes it harder to manage their intake, leading, most of the time, to their oblivion or intake at the wrong moment of the day.

Moreover, the participants also referred that with ageing, it became more difficult to remember information, and it is most likely they had forgotten to take their medication or to happen again in the future, clearly revealing a frequent problem and subsequently essential to address. Thus, the participants perceived the third suggested scenario well and considered it helpful to close fill out this issue.

It is essential to mention that according to the participants, the third scenario should be adjusted to the eventuality of them not remembering whether they had already taken or not their pills, so avoid wrong dosage intake. Regarding this matter, they have suggested that the third scenario must be reinforced by an efficient usage of pillboxes that would allow the user to quickly and effectively verify whether the dose has already been taken.

In chronological terms, in the next stage of the research, the list of functional requirements for the *ProSeniorTV* service will be drawn up, taking into account the feedback presented by the seniors when the focus group took place.

7   Future Work

Since this is an introductory work, it is expected that we can prototype and validate a proactive personal information assistant embedded in the TV ecosystem in the subsequent research stages. We must also ensure that this solution is personalised and adequate for seniors. In this regard, initially, we will begin by defining a list of functional requirements for the service considering feedback from senior participants regarding the usage scenarios presented in the focus group session. Using that information, the solution will then be prototyped. Using its prototype, it will also be determined the importance of events held locally for the quality of life of the target audience (the elderly) and if the conceptualised solution effectively can lead to a significant improvement in seniors' participation.

Afterwards, the solution will be conceptualised by characterising the service's concept, components, and requirements. In the final stage of the investigation, as mentioned above, the prototyping and validation of the solution will be carried out.

We must mention that seniors' collaboration will be crucial during the investigation process. Hence, elderly participation will be needed in stages like defining interface elements and validating the prototype in terms of usability and user experience (UX). Considering this, it will be necessary the organisation of new focus group sessions with senior participants to guarantee that the idealised system meets the needs of this type of public.

Acknowledgements. This research is funded by the Fundação para a Ciência e a Tecnologia (FCT) through a PhD research grant with the reference 2021.08467.BD. It was conducted with the collaboration of USIDEC, which selected 6 of its students to participate in the focus group session.

References

1. Silva, T., Abreu, J., Antunes, M., Almeida, P., Silva, V., Santinha, G.: +TV4E: interactive television as a support to push information about social services to the elderly. Procedia Comput. Sci. **100**, 580–585 (2016). https://doi.org/10.1016/j.procs.2016.09.198

2. Abdi, J., Al-Hindawi, A., Ng, T., Vizcaychipi, M.P.: Scoping review on the use of socially assistive robot technology in elderly care. BMJ Open 8(2), e018815 (2018). https://doi.org/10.1136/bmjopen-2017-018815

3. INE: Projeções de População Residente 2080. Contudo, na Área Metropolitana de Lisboa e no Algarve a população residente poderá aumentar. Destaque informação à Comun. Soc., pp. 1–21 (2020)

4. Ferreira, S., Veloso, A., Mealha, Ó.: Sociabilidade Online e os Participantes Seniores (2013)

5. Silva, T., Mota, M., Hernández, C., De Abreu, J.F.: Automatic creation of informative TV videos to be delivered through iTV: A system architecture. Procedia Comput. Sci. 121, 584–591 (2017). https://doi.org/10.1016/j.procs.2017.11.077

6. Hu, Q., Lu, Y., Pan, Z., Gong, Y., Yang, Z.: Can AI artifacts influence human cognition ? The effects of artificial autonomy in intelligent personal assistants. Int. J. Inf. Manag. 56, 102250 (2021). https://doi.org/10.1016/j.ijinfomgt.2020.102250

7. De Abreu, J.T.F., Dos Santos Almeida, P.A.F., Da Silva, T.E.M.C.: iNeighbour TV: a social TV application to promote wellness of senior citizens. In: Information Systems and Technologies for Enhancing Health and Social Care, pp. 1–19. IGI Global (2013). https://doi.org/10.4018/978-1-4666-3667-5.ch001

8. Ajam, H., Mu, M.: A middleware to enable immersive multi-device online TV experience. In: TVX 2017 - Adjunct Publication of the 2017 ACM International Conference on Interactive Experiences for TV and Online Video, pp. 27–32 (2017). https://doi.org/10.1145/3084289.3089919

9. Boldy, D., Grenade, L., Lewin, G., Karol, E., Burton, E.: Older people's decisions regarding 'ageing in place': a Western Australian case study. Australas. J. Ageing 30(3), 136–142 (2011). https://doi.org/10.1111/j.1741-6612.2010.00469.x

10. O'Rourke, H.M., Collins, L., Sidani, S.: Interventions to address social connectedness and loneliness for older adults: a scoping review. BMC Geriatr. 18(1), 1–13 (2018). https://doi.org/10.1186/s12877-018-0897-x

11. Amaro, F., Gil, H.: The 'Info-(ex/in)-clusion' of the elderly people: remarks for the present and for the future. In: ED-MEDIA 2011–World Conference on Educational Multimedia, Hypermedia & Telecommunications, vol. 2011, no. 1, pp. 1024–1030 (2011)

12. Sgarbi, E., Borges, D.L.: Structure in soccer videos: detecting and classifying highlights for automatic summarization. In: Sanfeliu, A., Cortés, M.L. (eds.) CIARP 2005. LNCS, vol. 3773, pp. 691–700. Springer, Heidelberg (2005). https://doi.org/10.1007/11578079_72

13. Font-Jutglà, C., Mur Gimeno, E., Bort Roig, J., Gomes da Silva, M., Milà Villarroel, R.: Effects of mild intensity physical activity on the physical condition of older adults: a systematic review. Rev. Esp. Geriatr. Gerontol. 55(2), 98–106 (2020). https://doi.org/10.1016/j.regg.2019.10.007

14. Chun, A.: Medical and preoperative evaluation of the older adult. Otolaryngol. Clin. North Am. 51(4), 835–846 (2018). https://doi.org/10.1016/j.otc.2018.03.010

15. Glass, T.A., Mendes De Leon, C.F., Bassuk, S.S., Berkman, L.F.: Social engagement and depressive symptoms in late life: longitudinal findings. J. Aging Health 18(4), 604–628 (2006). https://doi.org/10.1177/0898264306291017

16. Spinney, J.E.L., Scott, D.M., Newbold, K.B.: Transport mobility benefits and quality of life: a time-use perspective of elderly Canadians. Transp. Policy 16(1), 1–11 (2009). https://doi.org/10.1016/j.tranpol.2009.01.002

17. Liu, J., Rozelle, S., Xu, Q., Yu, N., Zhou, T.: Social engagement and elderly health in China: evidence from the China health and retirement longitudinal survey (CHARLS). Int. J. Environ. Res. Public Health 16(2) (2019). https://doi.org/10.3390/ijerph16020278

18. He, S.Y., Thøgersen, J., Cheung, Y.H.Y., Yu, A.H.Y.: Ageing in a transit-oriented city: satisfaction with transport, social inclusion and wellbeing. Transp. Policy 97, 85–94 (2020). https://doi.org/10.1016/j.tranpol.2020.06.016

19. Munteanu, C., Salah, A.A.: Multimodal technologies for seniors: challenges and opportunities. In: The Handbook of Multimodal-Multisensor Interfaces: Foundations, User Modeling, and Common Modality Combinations, vol. 1, pp. 319–362 (2017). https://doi.org/10.1145/3015783.3015793

20. Buccoliero, L., Bellio, E.: The adoption of 'silver' e-health technologies: first hints on technology acceptance factors for elderly in Italy. In: ACM International Conference Proceeding Series, vol. 2014-January, pp. 304–307 (2014). https://doi.org/10.1145/2691195.2691303

21. Sarikaya, R.: The technology behind personal digital assistants: an overview of the system architecture and key components. IEEE Signal Process. Mag. **34**(1), 67–81 (2017). https://doi.org/10.1109/msp.2016.2617341

22. Lazic, A., Bjelica, M.Z., Nad, D., Todorovic, B.M.: Google assistant integration in TV application for android OS. In: 2018 26th Telecommunications Forum, TELFOR 2018 - Proceeding, pp. 1–4 (2018). https://doi.org/10.1109/TELFOR.2018.8612143

23. Fisher, M.J., Noll, A.M., Fisher, D.E., Fink, D.G.: Television. Encyclopedia Britannica (2020). https://www.britannica.com/technology/television-technology. Accessed 20 Oct 2021

24. Abreu, J.T.F.: Design de Serviços e Interfaces num Contexto de Televisão Interactiva (2007). http://hdl.handle.net/10773/1259

25. Almeida, P., Ferraz de Abreu, J., Fernandes, S., Oliveira, E.: Content unification in iTV to enhance user experience: the UltraTV project, pp. 167–172 (2018). https://doi.org/10.1145/3210825.3213558

26. Costa, C., Anido-Rifón, L., Fernández-Iglesias, M.: An open architecture to support social and health services in a smart TV environment. IEEE J. Biomed. Heal. INFORMATICS **21**(2), 549–560 (2017). http://hdl.handle.net/10216/12822

27. Rosa, M.J.V.: Os reformados e os tempos livres. Bnomics (2015). https://novaresearch.unl.pt/en/publications/os-reformados-e-os-tempos-livres. Accessed 18 Mar 2021

Design and Development of an Assisted Ball Positioning System for Soccer Matches with an HBBTV Server Integrated to a Haptic TV Glove Accessible to Visually Impaired People

Diego Villamarín[1]([✉]) [ID], Andrés Narváez[2]([✉]) [ID], José Manuel Menéndez[1]([✉]) [ID], and Julio Larco[2]([✉]) [ID]

[1] Universidad Politécnica de Madrid, Madrid, Spain
df.villamarin@alumnos.upm.es, jmm@gatv.ssr.upm.es
[2] Universidad de Las Fuerzas Armadas - ESPE, Sangolquí, Ecuador
{afnarvaez,jclarco}@espe.edu.ec

Abstract. Currently, although there are several developments that allow digital inclusion and accessibility of people with hearing or visual impairments to audio and video content through TV or any audiovisual streaming platform. These developments have not been sufficient and have not had the distribution and implementation that they should have. For example, there is still a latent problem with blind people who cannot follow a soccer game autonomously; they need an announcer to narrate the game with more details than an announcer for blind people. The objective of this work was to create a solution that by means of a semi-automatic supervised system, registers the position and route of the ball in a soccer field, using a design tablet that encodes its location in the form of vectors. These location vectors were generated by a remote server running a Python script and triggered by a Hybrid broadcast broadband TV server. The HbbTV server interacts with the TV user and when it receives an activation or activity start message from the user, the Python server sends the data to an Internet of Things (IoT) platform in the cloud, which in turn is connected to the haptic glove that uses haptic engines to generate vibrations that can be interpreted by the visually impaired with touch, thus making it possible to become an accessible and inclusive TV device for these vulnerable groups.

Keywords: Haptic Glove · HbbTV · IoT · Accessible TV · Inclusive TV

1 Introduction

Accessibility in TV is still one of the weak points in spite of the constant development of this telecommunications sector. TV broadcasting stations have evolved from analog broadcasts in black and white, through color broadcasts, and now with digital broadcasts with great capacity for transmission of audio, video and data content, including video with Ultra High Definition UHD 4K capabilities. Although on issues of accessibility for

M. J. Abásolo and G. F. Olmedo Cifuentes (Eds.): jAUTI 2021, CCIS 1597, pp. 85–102, 2022.
https://doi.org/10.1007/978-3-031-22210-8_6

people with some physical impairment, such as hearing or visual, there are some works that have promoted their digital inclusion on TV. For example, for people with hearing impairment, it supports closed captioning and subtitling, in some cases automatically generated by speech to text tools [1, 2]. It also favors the sign language used by some programs or news programs, including some initiatives to generate sign language automatically [3]. For blind people there is audio description, which is a complementary audio where there is an explicit description of what is happening in the scene [4]. Other initiatives, such as the European projects EasyTV [5] or HBB4ALL [6], present solutions focused on accessibility and, although some of these have already been implemented, they have not yet been deployed as a true integral solution, and in most cases they have remained as isolated developments without their implementation being mandatory and available in all video platforms to provide true inclusion to these people.

In the study of existing previous works [7], it has been determined that there are no immersive and interactive solutions that allow blind or visually impaired people to access in some way to follow or interpret the scenes that are occurring in a sequence of images or video. Although this has been partially solved with audio description, but it is not a solution that is always present in all audiovisual content, whether it is broadcast by traditional broadcast media or streaming broadband platforms. And in many cases, audio description could even end up being annoying for sighted people who are watching the content together with a non-sighted person.

In a previous work we presented the development of a haptic glove that receives certain information from TV scenes [7], encodes it into vectors and presents this information through vibrations of haptic motors that have the ability to generate different effects. For the case study, the applied solution was proposed to track the location of the soccer ball when a sports match is taking place. But, in this work, the tracking of the location of the ball and the generation of the location vectors was developed manually, that is to say, a video of a sports match was chosen and the sampling was done, previously, with an observer who took the data every 500 ms, then this information was used to generate the vibrations of this sports match.

Nowadays, the development of object recognition or positioning systems is a topic that is in constant progress [8]. Their implementation brings benefits to different areas, mainly to vulnerable sectors. In general, the systems already developed are limited to offer assistance of past events because they generate their vectors manually. The development of an assisted system for positioning a ball on a soccer field can open the door to several applications aimed at recording statistical data and providing accessibility services to visually impaired people, and even more so if the data generated are available on web servers.

HbbTV (Hybrid Broadcast Broadband TV), is the European hybrid television standard that aims to combine television broadcasts with broadband services [12]. It will be the technology that will allow us to integrate the data generated with television, and thus offer immersive and interactive services to visually impaired people.

For this reason, the objective of this project was to create a semi-automatic supervised system, which by means of an operator who is watching a soccer sporting event, either live or pre-recorded, tracks the position of the ball by means of a graphic tablet design, This can generate positioning vectors of the ball with the help of a graphic interface designed in a development platform that stores the data in a web server with HBBTV technology, which in turn connects to any IoT (Internet of Things) platform that sends the information in real time to the haptic glove.

The development of this system in the future expects to obtain reliable metrics of QoS (Quality of Services) to be able to interpret the events in real time; it can open the field towards different applications and services that can be implemented, either by automating it or developing new applications that can be used through digital television. With this, it is expected to improve the lifestyle of this vulnerable sector.

2 Materials and Methods

2.1 Accessible Haptic TV Glove

This section will briefly explain the methodology of operation of the haptic glove for Accessible TV, presented in a previous work [7]. The court was subdivided into 45 equal parts, as shown in Fig. 1. On the X axis (length) there are 5 sections, on the Y axis (width) there are 3 sections, and on the Z axis (height) there are also 3 sections. If the ball only moved at ground level there would only be a two-dimensional XY plane, and there would be 15 sections in the court. But as the ball is not always at ground level, the Z vector was created with 3 sections, which represent the height of the ball in this way having a three-dimensional plane, Z1 when the ball is at ground level, Z2 when the ball rises to the height of the players' head and Z3 when the ball exceeds the height of the players' head.

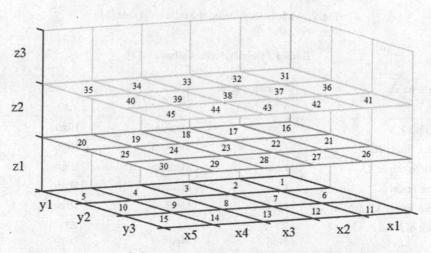

Fig. 1. Sectors of the soccer field that will be represented for ball tracking [7].

The 45 sectors or areas of the court are represented by 6 haptic motors with the ability to generate different vibration effects. Figure 2 shows the distribution of the motors on the right hand, where each motor is located on the fingertips and represents the 5 X sections of the court. Table 1 details the level of vibration generated by each of the motors to denote the location of the ball on the Y-axis. Finally, the location of the sixth motor on the back of the right hand with 2 vibration levels is observed to denote the height of the ball while a soccer match is taking place. It has already been mentioned that the sampling of the ball location was performed every 500 ms, but it is important to indicate that the vibrations are only generated when the ball or the play changes sector on the field.

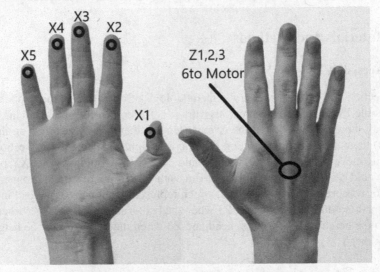

Fig. 2. Motors location on the right hand side [7].

Table 1. Detail of motor vibration [7].

Right hand	Vibration level		
	Y1	Y2	Y3
Thumb X1	Low	Medium	High
Index finger X2	Low	Medium	High
Middle finger X3	Low	Medium	High
Ring finger X4	Low	Medium	High
Little finger X5	Low	Medium	High
Back of hand Z	Z1 Null	Z2 Medium	Z3 High

Figure 3 shows evidence of the usability tests performed in [7]. The tests were conducted with 15 people with severe visual impairment who used and evaluated the haptic glove by means of surveys, using the Likert scale. The evaluation was subdivided into 4 stages: the first was to know their expectations and to give an explanation of its operation and previous training; the second stage was based on the usability, user experience and usefulness of the glove; the third stage of evaluation was focused on the ergonomics and comfort provided by the glove; and the last stage was to know the improvements that could be made and the future uses that could be given to the glove. The results of the study determined that the glove did meet the expectations it generated, that it did help to improve the understanding of a sporting encounter and that it was very well accepted by the users, most of whom would be happy to use it again. With this motivation, after these results, new challenges were posed, among them the generation of the vectors, at least in a first stage in a semi-automatic way.

Fig. 3. Usability evaluation tests of the haptic glove with blind people.

2.2 Ball Positioning Assist System

An Object Positioning System (OPS) has natural applications for tagging the environment. OPS could potentially be used to improve GPS, particularly when GPS errors are large or erratic. For this reason, an assisted system is sought in order to achieve the elimination of these errors and to obtain the relevant information for different uses of interactivity accessibility applications [8].

Currently, there are developed object recognition systems that are intended to be used in different applications, but in the field of sports, there is still little research on the subject. The analysis of the complexity of performance in soccer is, to this day, still a pending subject. The fluctuation of behaviors that occur during the game is a reality difficult to explain and predict [9].

The players and the ball are the most important objects in soccer videos. Their detection and tracking are motivated by various applications, such as event detection, tactics analysis, automatic summarization, and object-based compression. The methods for locating the ball and players in soccer videos can be divided into two groups: the first group uses fixed cameras (usually calibrated in advance) in a controlled environment; the second group uses only regular broadcast videos [10].

There are several systems, including artificial vision. Vision, both for a human being and for a computer, consists of two phases, which are acquisition and interpretation of an image. Thus, it is intended to simplify the system so that the acquisition is given by an operator and the interpretation of the data is given by the program [11].

In order to move forward with the development of the prototype of the haptic glove for accessible TV, as a first milestone we plan to make it semi-automatic, and it is the main objective of this work, as already mentioned. To achieve this milestone, the most feasible was to use a graphic tablet design that gives a great facility to track the ball on a soccer field and that adapts to our need, because with the buttons that has its digital sphere allows us to emulate the position in height Z1, Z2 and Z3, as shown in Fig. 4.

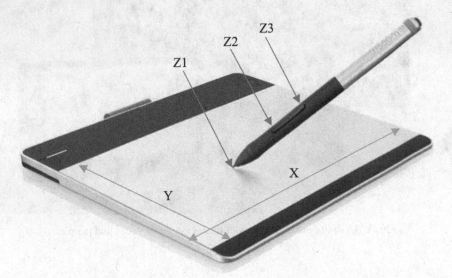

Fig. 4. Graphic tablet used to indicate the movement of the ball on the soccer field.

In order to reflect this movement and encode it automatically, a Python script was created. This code identifies or interprets the location of the pointer in pixels of the screen being used, and these pixels are transformed into the vectors we need to send them and then be reflected in the vibrations of the haptic engines. The code is made in a generic way to interpret the location of the pointer, so it is not essential to have a graphic design tablet like the one in Fig. 4. It could be replaced by the mouse or the pad of the PC being used, although due to the ease and precision provided by the device it would be optimal to use a tablet like the one in Fig. 4 to track the ball. The device used was a Wacom Intuos Creative Pen & Touch Tablet.

Figure 5 shows the graphic interface that generates the vectors according to the tracking of the location of the ball on the court. Figure 5 also shows that the pointer is in the location X3, Y2, Z1. It also provides information of the pixels in X & Y, the point or sector it represents according to the distribution that was in Fig. 1, and finally shows the time elapsed since the start of the tracking. The results of this implementation allow us to meet the objective of generating these vectors semi-automatically and without delays, since it practically does it in real time, and that was an important factor to integrate with the haptic glove, which will be detailed in the next section of results.

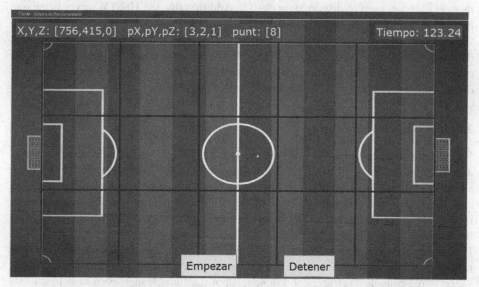

Fig. 5. Graphical interface for tracking ball location on the soccer field.

2.3 HbbTV Server

Another challenge facing the development of the glove is the means of dissemination or transmission of the vectors. Among the proposals is to send them encrypted in the Transport Stream (TS) of the TV transmission data stream [7], but the challenge is that all receivers should have the ability to interpret these metadata and be able to integrate with the glove. In the future, this would be an optimal solution since the data would travel together with the audio and video packets and could be easily synchronized, although it would require that the TV receiver had an integrated system capable of interpreting this information and generating the relevant output signal for the glove.

Another proposal was to choose an interactivity platform that could send this information or, in turn, alert that the video of the soccer match that is being attended has immersive content to synchronize with the haptic glove.

Hybrid Broadcast Broadband TV (HbbTV) is an industry standard that provides an open, technology-neutral platform that combines services delivered via broadcast with broadband Internet access services [12]. We chose to work with an HbbTV server because it is a standard that has become established and is gaining ground, even outside Europe. HbbTV in our case will be used as a gateway to the application. It sends the necessary information to announce that there is the possibility of accessing immersive content for the visually impaired through the haptic glove, and provides the steps that must be followed to link to this content. Once the end user's assistant, which would be the blind person who has the glove, accepts the start of the vibration reception, the glove will start receiving the vibration information reflecting the location of the ball on the soccer field. To have this graphical interface displaying the information to the HbbTV user, HTML5 is used to display it on the TV. Additionally, the HbbTV server is the one that stores the location of the ball, through a Python script and the use of websockets, which allow to receive the information from the vectors of our semi-automatic system, detailed in the previous section. When the HbbTV server receives the service activation order from the end user, it also acts as a gateway or bridge to the IoT server, which is directly connected to the IoT receiving device of the glove.

2.4   IoT Server or Platform

When something is connected to the internet it means it can send or receive information, and that ability to send or receive information makes things intelligent. That is what the so-called Internet of Things IoT is all about, extending access to the Internet beyond computers and smartphones to a wide range of devices or microcontrollers that can be in any appliance or device in the home or in our daily lives. And although we may not know it, more and more devices in our homes already have an Internet connection. For example, if you have a Smart TV at home, that device is already connected to the network and the same goes for our smart watch or any wearable device we now carry, video game consoles, refrigerator, kitchen, robot vacuum cleaner, even switches, lights or smart sockets with a microcontroller that allows WiFi connection and access to the network.

With the rise of the Internet of Things, there is also a variety of IoT platforms [13], including some of free access, which allow access to various resources, to control one or more devices with different access technologies, to collect information and display it on a dashboard for data analytics, etc. For the development of the glove we worked with the low-cost microcontroller containing a WiFi module ESP8266, which allows us to easily connect to the Internet through the development of Arduino or Python scripts. From a variety of platforms analyzed, we tested Thinger.io and Adafruit.io because both provide the necessary libraries to work with the ESP8266 quickly and easily, the service is in the cloud and is ideal for reading sensor data or control motors in real time, although with certain restrictions, for example, with the number of data sent per minute limited in its free version. But for our purposes it can be adapted without any problem. Of course, you can always switch to a paid version or to another platform with better features.

3 Results

3.1 System Integration

For the integration of the solution, we analyzed which would be the most viable and easy way for the end user to access the content through the HbbTV platform. And the biggest challenge was undoubtedly to obtain a correct synchronization of the audiovisual content with the vibrations generated by the glove. In HbbTV it is feasible to have two devices that synchronize their audio and video content [14], through the Disco-very and Launch Protocol (DIAL), which is also used by Netflix and Google's Chromecast to broadcast their content from a main device to a second device. The same happens in HbbTV: there is a first device or main screen that discovers a second companion device or second screen, and launches its content to it. In our case, analogously to the second screen, we wanted the glove to become an IoT companion device or gadget for TV, obviously with its limitations, since the glove does not reach the resources of a second screen. And precisely because of this limitation, in the hardware of the glove, it was decided that the haptic device controlled by the ESP8266 would simply connect to an IoT server and receive the sequence of vectors that generate the haptic vibrations in the glove.

In the first tests carried out even without end users, encouraging results were obtained without noticing a considerable delay that generates a desynchronization between the audiovisual content and the vibrations received, taking into account that there will be a delay not only in the reception but also in the generation of the vector, since there is an operator who is tracking the ball on the court. It should be noted that, from the experience of previous work [7] in the evaluation of results, the desynchronization or delay that exists is very difficult to perceive for a blind person, even more so if it is of small times of one or two seconds.

Figure 6 shows the general scheme of how the integration of the positioning system explained in the previous section was achieved, with the HbbTV server which, apart from being the gateway for the application, is transformed or acts as a bridge or gateway to the IoT server through the use of websockets. In turn, this IoT server is always connected to the accompanying device or haptic glove that will emit its vibrations according to the information it receives. It is important to mention that the operator or generator of the location of the ball can be in a network independent of the network where the end user of the glove is located. In fact, with a single operator that generates the ball tracking vectors in an HbbTV server could have the necessary information for hundreds or thousands of end users to have access to it, since it would depend on the number of blind people who have the haptic glove accessible for TV, assuming that, if HbbTV is used, the information goes by DTT (Digital Terrestrial Television), which is a broadcast system that would have a large audience and high reach. There is also the possibility that any person who is accompanying a blind person and shares the same network, becomes the operator of this semi-automatic system, thus allowing his companion to enjoy and share the sports match in a more immersive way with the tracking of the ball through haptic vibrations in the glove.

To better detail the diagram of the Integrated Positioning System with HbbTV and the Haptic Glove for Accessible TV, we will start by describing what the Assisted Ball

Position Generation System does, this is a program developed in Python that we have it running on a remote server with a public address which can be accessed from any browser. When the remote server executes the Python script, a graphical interface is displayed on the screen as shown in Fig. 5, where the operator can track the movement of the game within the sporting event, i.e. this script is the one that generates the location vectors within the court. In a second part of the scheme we can visualize the servers, although here could also be graphically the remote server that runs the Python script that we have already detailed in the first part, we have not included it because it is already included in the assisted system of ball position generation.

Let's start by detailing the function of the HbbTV server, this is the one that contains the gateway or the one that triggers the sending of data to the IoT server, ie is responsible for presenting on the viewer's screen information indicating that there is interactive or immersive content for TV accessible to visually impaired people. Then, when the blind

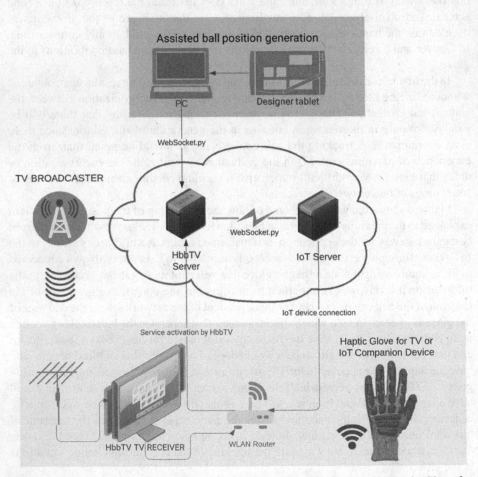

Fig. 6. Diagram of the Integrated Positioning System with HbbTV and the Haptic Glove for Accessible TV.

person's companion or assistant sees this, he/she can inform the blind person that this service is available and that he/she can put on the haptic glove to receive this information if he/she wishes. For this, and according to the acceptance and predisposition to receive this information by the blind person, the assistant or companion must interact with the TV and accept to receive the interactive content in the glove that the blind person should have previously put on. When the blind person has accepted to receive the immersive content through the remote control of the TV, the HbbTV server will send the data being generated by the remote server through the operator, i.e. at that moment the remote server will send the data to the IoT server, which in turn was previously configured in the haptic device to receive such information.

Finally, with the integration achieved with this system, a final testing stage was carried out in which the main objective was to make an evaluation in a real scenario with a blind person and an operator in order to have results and metrics that allow us to know if the system can be used in live or pre-recorded matches, where the generation of the vector is done attending any sporting event and at that same moment without further delay the blind person receives the vibrations of the haptic glove with the location of the ball. The results of this evaluation in a real scenario will be presented in the following section.

3.2 Evaluation Results in Real Scenario

The methodology to achieve this was as follows. We needed a TV showing any soccer match, we had an operator that is a person who attends the soccer match and live is tracking the location of the ball by a graphic tablet design connected to a PC in the case of not having a graphic tablet, it is also possible to track the ball using the mouse and keyboard of the PC, this real-time tracking is generating the vectors that are sent to the IoT server. On the other hand, we had a blind person, he is a 19-year-old boy who is beginning his university studies, he lost his vision at the age of 12. He was wearing the haptic glove on and receiving information from the IoT server, this information is reflected in vibrotactile movements in the haptic glove and also on the table we placed a court printed on paper with several signals that generated a sense of high relief, basically with these signals we marked the contour of the court and the 15 sectors of the court in the XY axes, this helped us so that the blind person could give us feedback on what he was interpreting from the vibrations he was receiving. In addition, we had a PC with the IoT server interface that showed us the value of the vector in decimal and with that we could identify that there were no delays and that it was receiving the correct information. Figure 7 shows the test scenario with all the details mentioned above.

The greatest difficulty was to propose the necessary metrics to quantify and measure the synchronization of the system. The first metric was latency, which is nothing more than the sum of time delays produced by the propagation delay of data or packets in a physical network, which in turn allows us to measure the average delay generated by the system in this real scenario. And this latency in general is the only metric that could be objectively quantified.

And this measurement helped us to determine that the response of the system is practically in real time. On the other hand, in order to have a global metric of the correct functioning of the system and of the synchronism, we based ourselves on a more

Fig. 7. Real evaluation scenario.

subjective and qualitative measure where we evaluated the correct position of the ball in the court and the interpretation that the blind person had at the moment of receiving that information, This metric is subjective because it is very dependent on human error, both from the person who is generating the location of the ball when tracking in real time and also from the blind person who receives the vibrations and was giving us the feedback or the interpretation of the location of the ball according to the vibrations he received in his hand. So overall these metrics helped us to determine if there is a correct synchronization of the system.

Other metrics or network parameters were not evaluated because the bandwidth required is very low since the vector that is sent is simply a decimal data that varies only when there is a change in the location of the ball position on the court.

Next, we will detail the delays recorded in order to quantify them. To measure latency, we used the ping test, which measures in milliseconds [ms] the time it takes for your local connection to communicate with a remote computer on the IP network. The first delay that could be quantified is the time it took to connect to the remote server that runs the Python code to display the field with its regions or divisions and that allows tracking. Figure 8 shows the ping test made from the operator's PC to the python server with public IP http://137.184.216.50/. An average of 103 ms was obtained.

Fig. 8. Ping test to the remote python server.

Then a second ping test was recorded, between the remote Python server and the IoT server, one sends the vectors generated by the operator and the other receives them and in turn transmits them to the IoT device in our case the haptic glove. Figure 9 shows the results of the ping test and based on these results we could calculate an average of 0.805 ms, i.e. on average there is not even a millisecond delay, this because the two servers are in the United States.

Fig. 9. Ping between remote server and IoT server.

Finally, to complete the partial delays, a ping test was recorded between the local network of the haptic glove with the address of the IoT server, as shown in Fig. 10 the average delay is 20 ms, i.e. we also have a super low delay time because this server is dedicated to IoT and has an adequate processing capacity to provide a low latency in its connection.

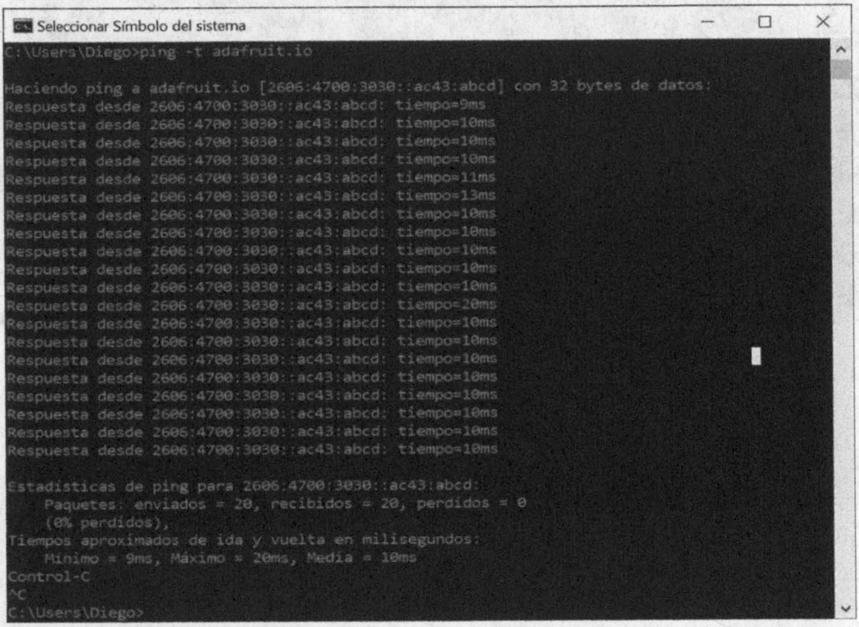

Fig. 10. Ping entre el guante y el servidor IoT.

In order to make a more detailed analysis, Table 2 shows a summary of the ping test records and shows the summation that would represent the total system latency metric.

Table 2. System latency

Partial delays	PING test metrics		
	Min [ms]	Max [ms]	Ave [ms]
Delay between PC and remote Python Server	81	230	103
Delay between remote server and IoT server	0.656	3.127	0.805
Delay between Glove and IoT Server	9	20	10
Sum or total latency	90.656	253.127	113.805

That is, we have 113.8 ms of latency or delay on average, this allows us to conclude that the delay is very low or in turn that the immediacy of communication is very good so we can say that we have a real-time system that has an adequate synchrony.

For the second part of this evaluation in a real scenario as we can see in Fig. 11, we propose to evaluate it in different plays or scenes where we were recording the play of the game, the movement or the generation of the vector location, and at the same time the feedback that the end user gave us about his interpretation of the vibrations received. In the image we can see, for example, that the operator is with the tracking cursor in the area of the arc on the left side, and in the grip on the table with the feedback indicators we can see the blind user with his finger on the area of the arc on the right side, and this is correct since the blind person is sitting against the operator, that is, he is located as if he were his reflection.

In order to have a metric that meets this objective, we propose a more than quantifiable parameter, a qualitative one, where we can say if the tracking of the play at a certain instant of time was right or wrong. Although, as mentioned before, this depended a lot on human errors and on the speed at which the operator made the tracking and, above all, on the speed at which the blind user interpreted the vibration and showed it to us inside the court with high relief signs.

Fig. 11. Evaluación final en escenario real.

In Table 3 we show the result of the evaluation, an acceptable performance is observed since there was a 76% of correct answers, which in reality as previously mentioned is quite subjective because according to the end user's statement there is a great difficulty at the moment of giving us the feedback because he must mentally place himself in the court and rely only on the signals in high relief.

Table 3. End-user interpretation performance evaluation

Moment of time	Play 1	Play 2	Play 3	Play 4	Play 5
t1	Right	Right	Right	Right	Right
t2	Right	Wrong	Wrong	Wrong	Wrong
t3	Right	Right	Right	Right	Wrong
t4	Right	Wrong	Right	Right	Right
t5	Right	Right	Right	Right	Right
Correctly interpreted movements	19				
Wrongly interpreted movements	6				
Successes percentage	76%				
Error percentage	24%				

As a final interpretation of this result it can be stated that, although the percentage of error that was measured in small samples of several plays of a soccer game is not very high, this is a very subjective result because for the end user it was very difficult in his brain to interpret the vibrations that he felt in his right hand and at the same time to be able to show them with his left hand. But according to his own version, it was very easy for him to simply interpret the movement and geo-localize in his brain, so surely this percentage of error is much lower than what we could measure and it will also depend on the ability and dexterity that the blind user develops in his brain.

4   Conclusions and Future Work

Based on the results obtained, it can be concluded that the solution of this semi-automatic system that registers the position of the ball on the court was feasible in order to allow the development of the haptic glove for Accessible TV. It is important the development of this type of proposals because they allow to provide real and feasible solutions to problems faced by thousands of people with visual impairment who do not have easy access to TV content. These initiatives are the ones that should be implemented to bridge the digital divide that exists for these vulnerable groups.

The solution that was proposed, with a platform or HbbTV server, could also be applied or replicated on another platform or interactivity standard such as GINGA, which is the interactivity middleware used in the Latin American ISDB-Tb standard. The challenges that remain are several, including the search to achieve a correct synchronization and further reduce delays, for which it is essential to know the limitations that exist and propose future work to propose feasible solutions.

In the evaluation in a real scenario, it was possible to have metrics that allow us to conclude that the low latency and the immediacy with which the vectors are generated with the location of the ball and the results are presented with the vibrations in the glove gives to validate that the system has no major synchronism problem and that it could be determined as a real-time and reliable system. In addition, it provides a quality of service and a pleasant user experience, which was also measured in previous works. One of the advantages of this assisted or semi-automatic system compared to a fully automatic system based on TV image analysis, is that it can also be easily adapted to applications in real soccer matches in any sports field.

In future work, it remains open the possibility of working with some artificial vision technique that allows to analyze the video in real time and identify the location of the ball and generate the vectors automatically. Another future work is to find the best way to transmit and receive these vectors, by encrypting the information as metadata within the data transport flow of any video standard, and expand the number of samples or users for evaluation and look for other ways to validate the results and metrics obtained.

References

1. Ang, F., Burgos, M. C., De Lara, M.: Automatic speech recognition for closed-captioning of Filipino news broadcasts. In: 2011 7th International Conference on Natural Language Processing and Knowledge Engineering, pp. 328–333 (2011). https://doi.org/10.1109/NLPKE.2011.6138219
2. Galvez, G.: Closed captioning and subtitling for social media. In: SMPTE 2017 Annual Technical Conference and Exhibition, pp. 1–10 (2017). https://doi.org/10.5594/M001804
3. de Araújo, T.M.U., et al.: Automatic generation of Brazilian sign language windows for digital TV systems. J. Braz. Comput. Soc. **19**(2), 107–125 (2012). https://doi.org/10.1007/s13173-012-0086-2
4. Ribalta, P.: Informe I/263-v2: Flujo de trabajo para la creación de Audiodescripciones, p. 8 (2011). http://anglatecnic.com/pdf/Flujo_Audiodescripcion.pdf
5. EasyTV Project: Easing the access of Europeans with disabilities EasyTV. A European horizon 2020 research project (2020). https://easytvproject.eu/
6. HBB4ALL Project: Hybrid broadcast broadband for all | HBB4ALL (2020). http://pagines.uab.cat/hbb4all/
7. Villamarín, D., Menéndez, J.M.: Haptic glove TV device for people with visual impairment. Sensors **21**, 2325 (2021). https://doi.org/10.3390/s21072325
8. Puneet, J., Manweiler, J., Roy, R.: Satellites in our pockets: an object positioning system using smartphones. In: The 10th International Conference, Low Wood Bay, Lake District, UK, p. 211. ACM Press. Obtenido de Duke University (2012)
9. Castellano, J.: Análisis de las posesiones de balón en fútbol. Eur. J. Human Mov. (2008) https://recyt.fecyt.es/index.php/ejhm/article/view/56325/34315
10. Huang, Y., Llach, J., Bhagavathy, S.: Players and ball detection in soccer videos based on color segmentation and shape analysis. In: Sebe, N., Liu, Y., Zhuang, Y., Huang, T.S. (eds.) MCAM 2007. LNCS, vol. 4577, pp. 416–425. Springer, Heidelberg (2007). https://doi.org/10.1007/978-3-540-73417-8_50
11. Ahumada Cortes, F.: Reconocimiento de Posicionamiento y Direccionamiento de Lego Robot a través de OpenCV. Obtenido de PONTIFICIA UNIVERSIDAD CATÓLICA DE VALPARAÍSO (2015) http://opac.pucv.cl/pucv_txt/txt-5000/UCD5098_01.pdf

12. Villamarín, D.: Estudio comparativo y de integración para las plataformas de televisión inter-activa europea HbbTV y latinoamericana Ginga. Trabajo Fin de Máster Universidad Politéc-nica de Madrid. Obtenido de Respositorio SENESCYT (2014). http://repositorio.educacion superior.gob.ec/bitstream/28000/1482/1/T-SENESCYT-00616.pdf
13. Campos, J.J.M., Marin, N.M.: Exploración de las plataformas IoT en el mercado para fomentar el conocimiento, buen uso y efectividad de los dispositivos IoT creados en la Facultad de Ingeniería y Ciencias Básicas de la Institución Universitaria Politécnico GranColombiano, p. 62 (2018)
14. Gómez, Á.L.: Desarrollo de servicios OTT síncronos mediante el estándar HbbTV 2.0.1 para TV digital. Trabajo Fin de Máster Universidad Politécnica de Madrid, p. 111 (2018)

Technologies, Services, and Applications for Interactive Digital TV

MixMyVisit – A Solution for the Automatic Creation of Videos to Enhance the Visitors' Experience

Pedro Almeida(✉) , Pedro Beça , José Soares , and Bárbara Soares

Digimedia, University of Aveiro, 3810-193 Aveiro, Portugal
{almeida,pedrobeca,josepsoares,bcjss}@ua.pt

Abstract. The experience of visitors in cultural spaces is not limited to the actual moments in that space. These institutions, like museums, seek to enrich the visitor's experience not only during but also after the visit. Creating solutions to capture memories of the visits can be a way to extend the experience. Therefore, this paper reports on a proposal of a system that automatically creates personalized memory videos of the visit to these spaces that may contribute to enrich the visitor's experience. Using simple devices, with NFC technology, the solution allows to identify the route of visitors in cultural places. For the solution, a bot was developed to interact with the visitor through a chat implemented in a social network (Facebook Messenger), allowing the visitor, through this chat, to share with the system its own content (photos or videos) aiming to be included in the video of the visit. Finally, a server-side video rendering engine, supported by the open-source ffmpeg software, and a responsive online video editor were implemented. The characteristics and main technical developments of this solution are presented in this paper. It also describes the evaluation carried with a functional prototype with 12 participants and the main results achieved. The solution proved to be captivating for the participants, with most of them considering having a great interest in the availability of such a solution in cultural spaces and/or museums. The evaluation also made it possible to obtain a set of improvement suggestions to be integrated in a future version aimed to be widely available to the public.

Keywords: Automatic video · Extend Museum Visit · Video editor · Enrich visitor's experience

1 Introduction

Cultural spaces such as museums, to best adapt their services to their audiences and ensure that they are positively affected in their contact with these spaces, need to understand the visitors' experience and develop solutions that improve that experience during the visit, but also to extend it after its conclusion. In this context, it is possible to observe that, "there is a lack of discussion about the museographic experience seen from the perspective of the visitor's behaviour" [1]. In fact, despite the concern with the experience provided by cultural spaces, there is not much investment in solutions to extend the experience after the visit.

© Springer Nature Switzerland AG 2022
M. J. Abásolo and G. F. Olmedo Cifuentes (Eds.): jAUTI 2021, CCIS 1597, pp. 105–118, 2022.
https://doi.org/10.1007/978-3-031-22210-8_7

The research presented in this paper describes a proposal to contribute to this area by presenting a system to identify the routes of visitors in cultural spaces and automatically create memory videos of the spaces visited, which allows an extension of the memory of the visit. This service, the MixMyVisit project, integrates several technologies and software modules to provide a service that automatically creates, without the need for visitor intervention, a personalized video of the visit, reflecting the locations where the visitor has been. If the visitor wants it is possible to get a more personalized video by sharing with the system, its ow videos or photos of the visit.

This system integrates low-cost devices equipped with NFC technology (bracelets that can cost less than 1 euro) that allow a simple method of identifying visitors. Additionally, it integrates three other software modules: i) a bot operated in a chat on a social network (Facebook Messenger) that allows textual interaction with visitors; ii) a module that detects the user's route, based on NFC receivers, and the contents received by the bot, identifies which contents are relevant to the visitor and to include in the video of his visit; iii) a module for the automatic creation of the video, its rendering and deliver to the visitor. These modules are described in detail in Sect. 3. In the following section a state of the art considering the visitor's experience is presented.

2   State of the Art

There are not many cultural spaces prepared to offer experiences that provide a complete visit that extends beyond the time spent in the cultural space. There are some research projects and prototypes that have already tried to extend the visit, as is the case of the LOL@ [2] and PEACH [3] projects, however, these projects only explore a limited area, in a non-interactive way. Kuflik, Wecker, Lanir, & Stock [4] defend this analysis stating that there are still "very few attempts to suggest a generic technological solution that goes beyond the isolated, face-to-face visit".

Despite these limitations, there are still relevant projects that explore concepts correlated with this proposal. This is the case of the PIL project, which was tested in an interior space and included user tracking methods using mobile devices - the "blinds" - and beacons placed in various areas of the museum. This system is able to generate a summary video, with customization limited to the visitor's name, gender and a photograph of the visitor, which follows the visitor's visit. The construction of the video is based on a compilation of pre-established contents associated with each of the exhibitions and pieces available according to the museum in question [5].

The LEGO House project automatically generates a video that evokes the memory of the visit, showing various LEGO buildings created by the visitor and photographs captured throughout the experience at specific museum locations. The location is guaranteed by a wristband with RFID technology that can be registered at the capture stations. At these stations the visitor can also take photographs or videos and add them to the visit [6]. At the end of the visit, the system considers all the content digitized and associated with the user, as well as their route in the visit, and generates a unique and personalized summary video with all the memories of the visit that can be obtained by accessing the LEGO HOUSE website. However, this system depends on the use of capture stations, not allowing videos or photos taken by the user to be included on their device.

3 The MixMyVisit Proposal

The MixMyVisit project is a collaboration between the University of Aveiro and Altice Labs with funding from Altice Labs@UA aimed at cultural public places such as museums to enrich the visitor's experience and memory of the visit. The MixMyVisit application intends to identify the visitor's paths in a cultural space and create an automatic and customizable video of the spaces' memory, allowing the visitor to share it on the social networks. It also allows the visitor to edit the video created in an online video editor, where the visitor can include additional content, change the order of video content, or delete any content from the video.

The system integrates NFC-based identification solutions through a wristband that tracks the paths of the visitor to identify the visited places and with that information decide the pre-recorded videos to be included in the video of the visit. In a differentiated feature regarding the state of the art, the visitor can communicate with the system via a chat bot, in a popular social network, allowing the visitor to share photos or videos that were captured during the visit in its own smartphone. At the end of the visit, the system compiles the pre-recorded video clips with the user generated content to provide a personalized video of the visit. The workflow of a visit is illustrated in Fig. 1.

| Visitor | Museum | Get writsband at reception and scan it in tablet | Authenticate and start visit via chatbot | Register content of location via scanning bracelet | Add user content by uploading to chatbot | User ends visit when scanning bracelet in station |

Fig. 1. The steps a typical user may do during a visit using the MixMyVisit solution.

The solution also allows for an anonymous use, not needing the visitor to use its own mobile device and identifying in any matter. In this case the visitor is not able to share its own videos or photos (since it relies in a chat conversation) and uses the wristband as an identification device all along the visit. In the end of the visit by presenting wristband the visitor gests a QR-code that can be scanned to get the URL of the final video.

3.1 Architecture

The solution integrates several modules dedicated to specific features, that architecture is presented in Fig. 2. Regarding the identification of the visitor, it relies in an NFC wristband that the visitor uses during the visit and interacts with it in portable devices (e.g. tablets) with NFC sensors. These devices are placed in specific spots of the cultural space, allowing visitors to interact with them via the NFC bracelet (no touch needed) to check in the visitor in that spot of the visit. One server-side module (3) manages the data received from the mobile devices and updates the visit of the user, which is stored in a SQL database (3.1), adding new spots or contents to the visit. Additionally, the service incorporates one chatbot (5) integrated in a social network for the user to interact with and obtain information practically and rapidly via text commands. The architecture is also composed of a server-side video engine (4) that, based on data of the route taken by the user, will gather the contents, videos, or images, of the route in question and automatically edit and build one video representing the visit and shares it with the visitor. Finally, the architecture also includes two modules (1 and 2) dedicated to the frontend of the solution which represent the website and mobile app to be available in the portable devices.

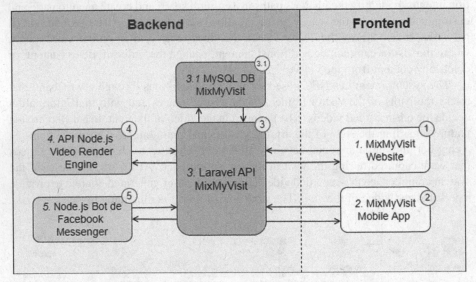

Fig. 2. Visual representation of the architecture modules related to the MixMyVisit solution.

3.1.1 MixMyVisit API

The central module of the architecture is a web API which communicates and interacts with a SQL database that stores all the data from the users, their visits, and its contents. This API was developed in PHP and Laravel framework. The API can be characterized being a REST API, following an MVC (model, view, controller) design pattern, which contains different interactive endpoints that store, update, read and delete data of the database. It is from these modules that the remaining elements of the architecture, like the website, mobile App, or video render engine, receive the required data for their interfaces or for their scripts to work correctly, either data related to the users, visits or contents.

3.1.2 Frontend Modules

The modules that compose the frontend interface of the solution are the website and the mobile application. Focusing on the website, it is developed with React.js framework and with a couple of website maintenance libraries (e.g., detecting if the user is authenticated or enabling the video editor features or for the development of a consistent visual interface build with reusable components). As referred the features available on the website include a video editor (Fig. 3), allowing a visitor to make changes to the contents (duration and textual comments) of the visit.

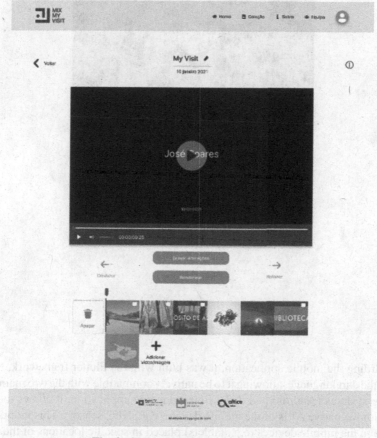

Fig. 3. The video editor on the website.

Additionally, the user can find a list of all previous visits done in the system (Fig. 4).

Fig. 4. The history of visits page.

Regarding the mobile application, it was built with the Flutter framework, which is based in the dart language, allowing it to be natively compatible with the two main mobile operating systems (Android and iOS). Being a native application, it allows to interact easily with the native APIs of the mobile device (e.g., NFC sensor). This mobile app is available in the mobile devices (e.g., tablets) placed in specific locations of the cultural space allowing the user to interact with it by approaching the wristband. After scanning the wristband, the user is presented with the options to see the registered locations in the visit, finish or cancel the visit (Fig. 5: middle). In case the user carries a wristband, which is not yet associated with a visit, a specific screen will be displayed with information to the user (Fig. 5: left). In some situations, the user is presented with a QR-code to be scanned, namely, to scan and start interacting with the Facebook Messenger chatbot or to scan to go to the online video editor (Fig. 5: right).

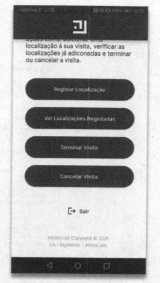

Fig. 5. Sample screens of the mobile application (left: initial screen after scanning NFC tag not associated with any visit, in the middle: the main menu of the visit, right: QR-code presented to redirect the user to an online video editor).

3.1.3   Video Render Engine

To allow the server-side processing of the video, a backend structure of Node.js was used, together with the framework Express and with different libraries for the configuration of the environment (e.g., fn, fluent-ffmpeg libraries). The solution for the creation of the videos was conceived based on the open-source component, ffmepg, used for processes like encoding, decoding of audio files, images, and videos. In addition, ffmpeg also handles the manipulation of files of different types, editing features and video transitions (Fig. 2: 5). The procedure of processing a video contains a couple of actions to manage audios and transitions in the video and provide the complete result to the user (Fig. 6).

The system is structured in two backend endpoints, one to receive the different requests for the completion of visits, via web-sockets and a simple http request, and another that receives the requests for completion and oversees executing them, including queue functionalities for proper handling of the video render tasks. The video processing architecture is built with a strong emphasis on all the different possible scenarios while executing this process, especially when it comes to errors with an error handling system that is simultaneously useful to give feedback for the users and for the developers to catch possible bugs.

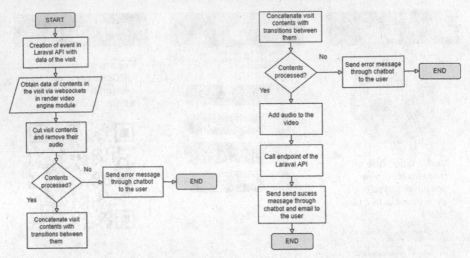

Fig. 6. Flowchart representing the process of rendering a visit video in the video render engine module (read from left to right vertically).

3.1.4 Chat Bot

To guarantee wider access to all potential visitors, a chat bot that allows for a simple text communication with the system in any device was developed and the Facebook Messenger network was chosen due to its great popularity and adherence to the general population. To interact with the bot, the users can scan a personalized QR-code presented to the visitor at the beginning of the visit that allows for a simple way to start a chat with MixMyVisit bot, enter a random PIN provided to the visitor and establish the identification of the Messenger account associated with a unique wristband (Fig. 7: left). A Facebook module dedicated to the MixMyVisit application was created, where different functionalities were activated to allow to interpret the content of messages sent to the chat of that same page, being able to distinguish between simple commands (e.g. ask for the video render) or the upload of images and videos to be included in the video of the visit (Fig. 7: right). After this first step, it was necessary to establish a back-end server to receive the contents of the messages and, subsequently, trigger events according to the received messages. It also includes notification mechanisms for warning the visitor of the completion of tasks, via Facebook Messenger API. The bot is managed in a server module created in Node.js (Fig. 2: 5).

4 Evaluation

To gather preliminary evaluation results regarding the developed solution, an evaluation was prepared based on 2 fundamental moments. The first moment, in an intermediate stage of development, was carried out with two experts in the museography area, specifically with expertise in multimedia developments for this field. The experts were able to try a prototype of the system and understand its features. They considered that the effectiveness of this system would be directly related to its ease of use, including the

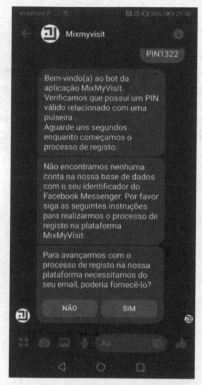
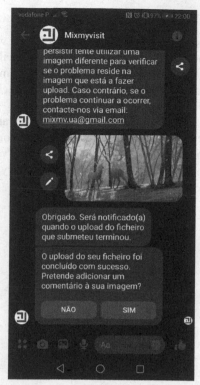

Fig. 7. Chatbot interaction examples (left: registering the user in the visit, right: the visitor uploading an image to be added to the visit).

interactions with the wristband, chatting with the chat bot and interacting with an online video editor, so that all types of visitors can understand and use it quickly. The importance of personalized videos was also highlighted, since it is a distinctive feature and an extra motivation, according to the experts, for users to share their videos on social networks [7].

The second evaluation moment came after the completion of the functional prototype and was based on a field evaluation with 12 participants. Due to the limitations associated with the Covid-19 pandemic, it was not possible to carry out this evaluation in a museum, so, to overcome this adversity, a field study was prepared based on the visits usually promoted by the University of Aveiro to its buildings and associated architecture. The evaluation tests were carried out with 12 participants including users of different age groups (18 to 58 years old) and genders. The participants visited the university campus interacting with the application, with the chat bot and incorporated content, photos, or videos, captured by them in their visits. Data collection instruments included a characterization questionnaire and a post-assessment questionnaire.

4.1 Results

As referred, the MixMyVisit solution was tested with 12 participants aged between 18 and 58 years old. There were both male and female participants and their technology literacy and frequency of use of social media was quite diverse, with participants ranging from being completely experienced technology users to others who aren't so proficient in this field.

Firstly, it was attempted to understand the visitors' evaluation on the way the system detected the routes through the detection of the wristband. The answers were, in general, positive, −41,7% (n = 5) said it was "very easy", 50% (n = 6) considered it was "easy" and only 8,3% (n = 1) felt it was "very difficult" (Graph 1).

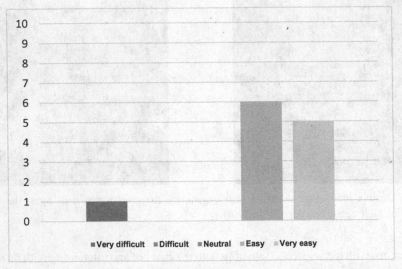

Graph 1. The easiness of the bracelet's/wristband's detection solution.

The post-visit questionnaire was also intended to assess the easiness identified in various tasks directly related with the interaction with the system throughout the visit (Graph 2). These aspects were initiating the conversation with the Messenger bot, sending content through the conversation with the bot and asking for the final video of the visit, either through the Messenger bot or through the wristband detection device. The answers to these questions were mostly very positive, with 6 to 8 participants always identifying all these aspects as easy or very easy. In all these questions, only 1 participant classified these tasks as being difficult.

Regarding the online video editor, the users who used it gave positive feedback on its relevance and ease of use (Graph 3). When it comes to the appeal of the online video editor, only 2 participants found it "neutral", while other 3 considered it "appealing" and there was even one other user who evaluated it as "very appealing". The other 6 opted for "non applicable", since they didn't choose to use the online video editor during the visit (it is not mandatory, users may use it if they want to change something on the automatic created video).

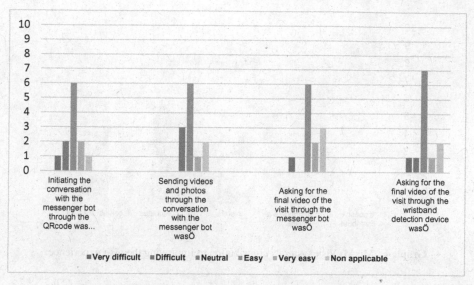

Graph 2. Ease of interaction with various aspects of the system.

The participants were also questioned specifically about the ease of use of the online video editor and the results were very similar, with overall positive answers. Even though 3 participants considered this was a "neutral" aspect, the 3 other users thought it was "easy" or "very easy" to use.

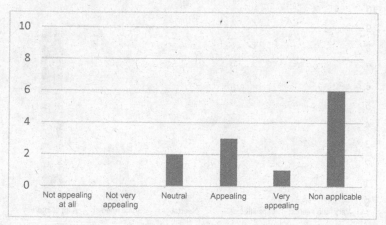

Graph 3. Evaluation of the online video editor.

When asked about this system's contribution for the automatic generation of personalized videos to improve the experience of visiting cultural spaces, 33,3% (n = 4) considered that this system contributes a lot to this improvement, 50% (n = 6) considered that it contributes to the improvement and 16,7% (n = 2) felt that this contribution was neutral (Graph 4).

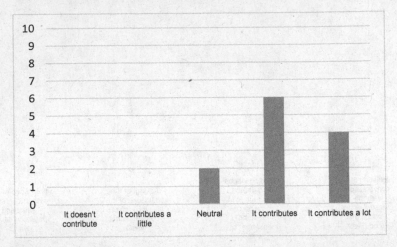

Graph 4. MixMyVisit system's contribution to improving the visit experience.

At the end of this questionnaire, participants were asked on what would be their level of interest in a system that would automatically create a personalized video of the visit to a cultural space based on the visited areas and the responses were entirely positive, with 75% (n = 9) considering being "very interested" and 25% (n = 3) identifying "some interest" in this solution (Graph 5).

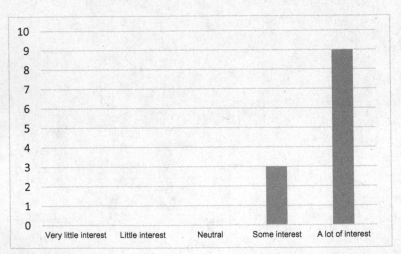

Graph 5. Participants' level of interest in a system such as the one proposed through MixMyVisit (after the visit).

5 Conclusions

The development of the MixMyVisit application required the integration of different technologies and structures to create a simple way to offer visitors to cultural spaces, such as museums, a personalized video reflecting the visit made. The team managed to implement a solid prototype that gained positive feedback from expert assessment and a group of potential end-users in field assessment tests. The experts highlighted the need for a simple and practical solution and the importance of being able to personalize the videos. These requirements are met in the developed solution by supporting the upload of visitor-generated content, via the chat bot, and by the non-intrusive method of tracking used to determine the visitor's path. On the other hand, the results of the field study with 12 participants, an intentional and non-representative sample, carried during a visit to the architecture highlights of the University of Aveiro campus, revealed that the majority considered the concept of creating a memory video, preferably personalized, for a visit to a cultural space to be interesting and relevant. Some aspects that can be improved were also highlighted to encourage visitors to share their video on social networks and edit it in the online video editor on the MixMyVisit website. Although the group of participants in the evaluation was small, it allowed to gather some indications that can be validated in future moments of evaluation, namely with a greater number of users.

The process of developing the technological solution and the evidence resulting from the first evaluation phase allow, on the one hand, to validate the technical implementation and, on the other hand, to conclude on the relevance of this type of solution for the experience of visiting a cultural space, encouraging the team in continuing the development and preparing the next assessment steps. The team is carrying further improvements on the solution to make it even less intrusive, more practical, and customizable, potentially providing an even more enriching experience for users. The optimized prototype will be evaluated in other scenarios with different audiences to further validate the technical solution, its relevance to the visitor and the user experience provided.

Acknowledgments. This work is part of the MixMyVisit project developed by Digimedia – University of Aveiro and Altice Labs with funding from Altice Labs @UA.

References

1. Liu, S., Yang, Y., Shafi, M.: A study of museum experience evaluation from the perspective of visitors' behavior. In: Xu, J., Ahmed, S.E., Cooke, F.L., Duca, G. (eds.) ICMSEM 2019. AISC, vol. 1002, pp. 683–693. Springer, Cham (2020). https://doi.org/10.1007/978-3-030-21255-1_52
2. Umlauft, M., Pospischil, G., Niklfeld, G., Michlmayr, E.: LoL@, a mobile tourist guide for UMTS. Inf. Technol. Tour. **5**(3), 151–164 (2003). https://doi.org/10.3727/109830503108751108
3. Stock, O., et al.: Adaptive, intelligent presentation of information for the museum visitor in PEACH. User Model. User-Adap. Inter. **17**(3), 257–304 (2007). https://doi.org/10.1007/s11257-007-9029-6

4. Kuflik, T., Wecker, A.J., Lanir, J., Stock, O.: An integrative framework for extending the boundaries of the museum visit experience: linking the pre, during and post visit phases. Inf. Technol. Tour. **15**(1), 17–47 (2014). https://doi.org/10.1007/s40558-014-0018-4
5. Lanir, J., Kuflik, T., Zolantz, I., Lanzet, U.: Personalized video summary of a museum visit (2013). https://www.semanticscholar.org/paper/Personalized-Video-Summary-of-a-Museum-Visit-Lanir-Kuflik/e50fc5f2e665f8085f075afa05094750412e93a2
6. LEGO® House - The world's best play date. https://legohouse.com. Accessed 31 Mar 2021
7. Almeida, P., Beça, P., Soares, J., Soares, B.: MixMyVisit - enhancing the visitor experience through automatic generated videos. In: IMX 2021 - Proceedings of the 2021 ACM International Conference on Interactive Media Experiences, pp. 233–236 (2021). https://doi.org/10.1145/3452918.3465500

Selection of Configurable Computer Module Applied to Home Automation and Interactive Digital Television

Joaquín Danilo Pina Amargós(✉) ⓘ, Enrique Ernesto Valdés Zaldívar, Juan Carlos Cruz Hurtado, and Raisa Socorro Llanes

Universidad Tecnológica de La Habana "José Antonio Echeverría" (CUJAE), Havana, Cuba
{jpina,raisa}@ceis.cujae.edu.cu,
{enrique.valdes,juan.cruz}@cime.cujae.edu.cu

Abstract. Advances in information technologies (IT) are achieving technological convergence in most scenarios of everyday life. However, these advantages are not fully exploited and each application scenario, such as digital television and smart rooms, uses different computing devices that increase dependence on foreign suppliers, increase production or marketing costs and cannot be reused in other similar scenarios, nor to expand their possibilities and lengthen their obsolescence period. This situation is further aggravated in the context of Cuba as a country blocked and besieged by the government of the United States of America. The medical equipment and tourism industries are current examples of these limitations by not being able to buy electronic supplies, seeing their commercialization limited or not being able to offer a greater convenience of infommunication services to their customers. This article aims to identify a computing module that can be adapted to different scenarios by modular coupling of expansion interfaces to achieve connection with different peripherals (such as: USB, RF input, HDMI output, Ethernet Interface, WiFi and others). The scenarios are presented: digital terrestrial TV decoder in various models and home automation. As a result of technological convergence, software components can be reused to develop human-computer interactivity in various emerging technological scenarios in a continuity of the present work.

Keywords: Internet of things · Home automation · Computing module

1 Introduction

Advances in information technologies (IT) are achieving technological convergence in most scenarios of everyday life [18]. Computing systems from the cloud

Supported by Perez-Guerrero Trust Fund for South-South Cooperation (PGTF) United Nations Development Programme (UNDP) project INT/19/K08 and Ministry of Science, Technology and Environment of Cuba project PN223LH006-018.

M. J. Abásolo and G. F. Olmedo Cifuentes (Eds.): jAUTI 2021, CCIS 1597, pp. 119–132, 2022.
https://doi.org/10.1007/978-3-031-22210-8_8

to mobile phones and wearable devices connect with each other to provide people with interactive content and a wide variety of services that are presented in different representation formats [22].

However, these advantages are not fully exploited and each application scenario uses different computing devices that increase dependence on foreign suppliers, increase production and marketing costs and cannot be reused in other similar scenarios or to expand their possibilities so that their obsolescence period is prolonged. This situation is even more aggravated in countries blockaded and besieged by foreign powers such as the one suffered by Cuba due to the government of the United States of America [27]. The medical equipment and tourism industries are current examples of these limitations by not being able to buy electronic supplies, seeing their commercializations limited or not being able to offer a greater comfort of IT services to the sick or guests.

Based on this situation, this research work aims to identify computer modules that can be adapted to different scenarios through the modular coupling of expansion interfaces to achieve connection with different peripherals (such as: USB, RF input, HDMI output, RJ-45 Ethernet interface, WiFi and others) [14].

The principles that will guide this goal are: maximize technological sovereignty, minimize the cost of its production and allow technological convergence so that it can be reused in different scenarios [9]. The scenarios are presented: digital terrestrial TV decoder and home automation. Sovereignty refers to the design of the electronic components board, the operating system, component libraries and reusable softwares such as the web browser where the specific functionalities of the scenario addressed are implemented. For electronic components, different foreign, non-American suppliers would be identified, so as not to depend on a specific one and, above all, to minimize the effect of the extraterritorial laws of foreign powers.

2   Previous Works

A single-board computer (SBC) is a complete computer, built on a single board, containing microprocessors, memories, input/output devices and others that are required to complete a functional computer.

SBCs are increasingly being applied due to their low costs, ease of installation and maintenance, reduced energy consumption and small size, which makes it possible to reach hard-to-reach places [16,20,28]. The possibilities of these equipment grow even more by the digital interconnection of everyday objects what is known as the Internet of Things (IoT). Forecasts state that the IoT market is one of the fastest growing in the next decade with a 20% annual [2].

In addition to the possibilities as an isolated computer equipment, another scenario in which SBCs can be applied is in the creation of micro data centers to reduce costs and latency in responding to real IoT scenarios [1,5,6,21]. Security is an important aspect in this type of scenario and has been addressed with good results as is the case of [3]. Even in complex computer vision and digital signal processing scenarios there are applications with very good results [19]. Some works demonstrating real-time processing with voice message recognition have also been presented [4, 10]. In [11] an architecture composed of low-cost Single-Board-Computer clusters near to data sources, and centralised cloud-computing data centres is presented. This architecture demonstrated a reduction in energy consumption and installation and maintenance costs without losing response time in scenarios where high computing power is not required such as the presented traffic-system scenario.

The possibilities described above are in line with the Sustainable Development Goals of the 2030 Agenda of the United Nations Development Program [25]. Through its extensive application, low-income countries find a way to achieve the development of society in a friendly and sustainable way in its interaction with the environment.

As an example, some figures are presented that illustrate the magnitude of the generalization of these solutions for a low-income country and, with the particularity that it has been blocked by the government of the United States of America for more than 60 years [27].

There are 3.5 million households in Cuba with 2.7 million digital terrestrial TV (DTT) receivers installed [7]. In addition to the above, there are more than 150 thousand rooms in the tourist facilities. On the other hand, it stands as the telecommunications infrastructure, maintaining a steady increase with a mobile penetration of 6.6 million services on the internet, of which about 2 million are on the 4G network [12].

However, these interconnection possibilities are not being exploited to their full extent in proposed scenarios because both in DTT and home automation interactivity is null and the smart room capacity is practically nonexistent [24].

Taking into account the situation described above, the scenarios proposed for this work are as follows: multimedia center with interactive terrestrial digital television set-top box and smart room control center (home automation), see Fig. 1. Of course, as a result of technological convergence and the generality of SBCs, software components will be able to be reused to develop human-computer interactivity in various emerging technological scenarios such as: vital medical parameter monitor [15] and precision agriculture [17].

The analysis shown below is supported by the Government management system based on science and innovation proposed in [8].

3   Identified Application Scenarios

The identified scenarios are characterized as follows:

Media center, DTT decoder:
  - DTMB standard demodulator (GB 20600-2006) 6 MHz;
  - Standard definition digital TV set-top box (SDTV) that supports image formats 720 × 480i at 59,94 fps and 720 × 480p at 29,97 fps, video compression ISO/IEC 13818-2 (H.262 or MPEG-2 Part 2) MP@ML; ISO/IEC 14496-10 (H.264/AVC or MPEG-4 Part 10) MP@L3; IEEE Std. 1857TM-2013 (AVS1-P2) Jizhun Profile, Level 4.0.0.08.30, sound compression ISO/IEC 13818-3 Layer 2 (MPEG-2 Part 3 Layer 2);

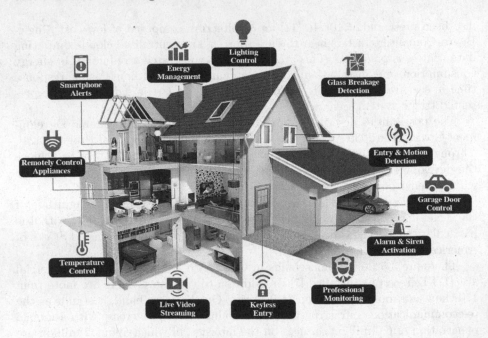

Fig. 1. Some functionalities present in home automation and smart room.

- High definition digital TV set-top box (HDTV) that supports image formats 1280 × 720p at 59,94 fps; and 1920 × 1080i at 59,94 fps, video compression HP@L4; IEEE Std. 1857^{TM}-2013 (AVS+ or AVS1- P16) Level 6.0.0.08.60, sound compression ISO/IEC 14496-3 (MPEG-4 Part 3 Subpart 4 AAC);
- RF input by F type female connector (ANSI/SCTE 02 2006);
- Video output by HDMI interface (version 1,2 or high);
- Infrared reader for remote control.

Control center for home automation and smart room [24]

- Ethernet IEEE 802.3 interface;
- Wifi IEEE 802.11 interface;
- Audio microphone to pick up voice commands;
- (Optional) Video output by HDMI interface (version 1,2 or high);

4   Proposed Solution

The general objective of this work proposes the development of a computing module of general-purpose type SBC with their software system that can adapt to different scenarios using the coupling modular interfaces expansion for the connection with various peripherals; under the premise of maximizing the technological sovereignty, to minimize the cost of production and allow for technological convergence so that it can be reused in different scenarios.

Taking into account the antecedents raised, an analysis of the existing SBCs was carried out. The study was limited to those with a price of around 50 USD so that they met the requirement that their cost of generalization had the lowest possible price. The main characteristics of the analyzed STBs are shown in Table 1 (see the reference photographs of each one in Figs. 2, 3, 4 5 and 6).

Table 1. Computing modules with an approximate cost of 50 USD (taken from the SBC Database https://hackerboards.com/).

SBC, Manufacturer	CPU	RAM	Interfaces	Year	Cost ($\approx$ USD Dec. 2021)
ODROID C4, Hardkernel Co. Ltd., KR	4× ARM Cortex-A55 2.0 GHz	4 GB DDR4	4× USB 2.0, micro-USB OTG, HDMI 2.0, 25× GPIO pins pins	2020	50
Raspberry Pi 4, Raspberry Pi Foundation, UK	4× ARM Cortex-A72 1.5 GHz	2-4-8 GB LPDDR4	2× USB 3.0, 2× USB 2.0, 2× HDMI 2.0, 40× GPIO pins, 7× GPIO pins	2019	55 (4 GB RAM)
Raspberry Pi Zero 2W, Raspberry Pi Foundation, UK	4× ARM Cortex-A53 1.0 GHz	512 MB LPDDR2	1× Mini-HDMI, 1× Micro-USB 2.0 OTG, 1× Camera Serial Interface, 40-pin GPIO Header	2021	15
Orange Pi 4, XunLong Software, CN	4× ARM Cortex-A53 2.0 GHz + 2× Cortex-A72 1.5 GHz	4 GB DDR4	2× USB 3.0 + 2× USB 2.0 + 1× tipo C, HDMI 2.0, 40× GPIO pins, 7× GPIO pins, MIC	2019	50
PocketBeagle, BeagleBoard, USA	1× ARM Cortex-A8 1.0 GHz + 1× Cortex-M3 Coprocessor + 2× PRUs	512 MB DDR3	1× USB OTG, 2× 36-pins GPI	2018	45

As can be noted, the STBs have similar characteristics, with connectors for various peripherals via USB and HDMI and all allow extension via general-purpose input and output connectors (GPIO). However, the decision leans towards the *Orange Pi 4* considering that the manufacturer does not rely directly on North American components such as its Rockchip RK3399 processor. In addition, the *Orange Pi 4* is the only module that has a built-in microphone so it can

Fig. 2. A single board computer of the brand ODROID model C4.

Fig. 3. A single board computer of the brand Raspberry Pi model 4.

Fig. 4. A single board computer of the brand Raspberry Pi model Zero 2W.

Fig. 5. A single board computer of the brand Orange Pi model 4.

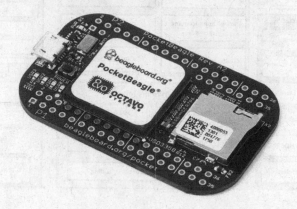

Fig. 6. A single board computer of the brand PocketBeagle.

respond to home automation applications. The block diagram of the processor is shown in Fig. 7 where it can be verified that it meets the requirements of the scenarios raised in this work.

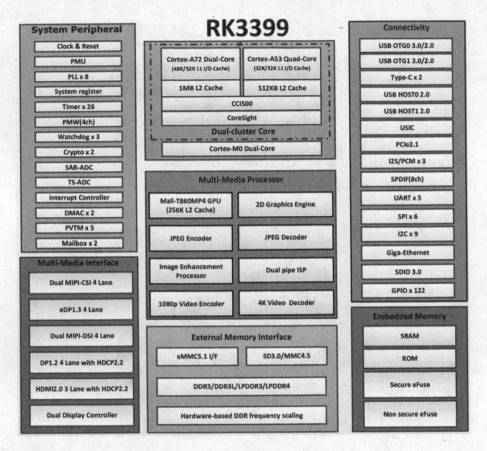

Fig. 7. Block diagram of the Rockchip RK3399 processor contained in the *Orange Pi 4* SBC [13].

The professional version RK3399Pro is a low power, high performance processor for computing, personal mobile internet devices and other smart device applications. Based on Big.Little architecture, it integrates dual-core Cortex-A72 and quad-core Cortex-A53 with separate NEON coprocessor. Equipped with one powerful neural network process unit (NPU), it supports mainstream platforms in the market, such as caffe, tensor flow, and so on. Many embedded powerful hardware engines provide optimized performance for high-end application. RK3399Pro supports multi-format video decoders and encoders. Embedded 3D GPU makes RK3399Pro completely compatible with OpenGL ES1.1/2.0/3.0/3.1, OpenCL and DirectX 11.1. Special 2D hardware engine with MMU will maximize display performance and provide very smooth operation.

An example of the modular extension can be seen in the incorporation of the digital TV receiver. Figure 8 shows an SBC with an expansion card connected to receive the DTT signal modulated in DVB-T/T2.

Fig. 8. A SBC *Raspberry PI 4* model B with an expansion card connected to receive the DTT signal modulated in DVB-T/T2.

For simpler scenarios the proposed solution can be integrated with low-cost microcontrollers such as the ESP32-C3 (see Fig. 9). ESP32-C3 series of SoCs is an ultra-low-power and highly-integrated MCU-based solution that supports 2.4 GHz Wi-Fi and Bluetooth LE. The block diagram of ESP32-C3 is shown in Fig. 10.

Fig. 9. An ESP32-C3 microcontroller.

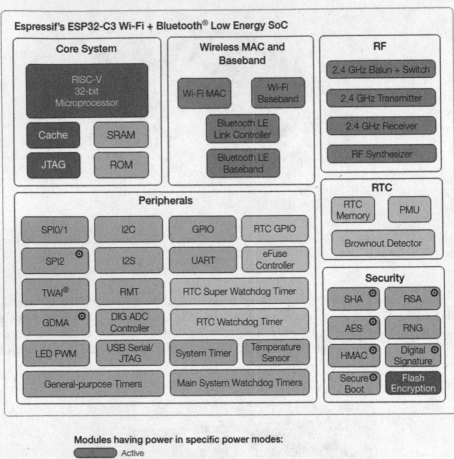

Fig. 10. Block diagram of the Espressif's ESP32-C3 microcontroller [23].

The ESP32-C3 series has the following highlights:

– A complete WiFi subsystem that complies with IEEE 802.11b/g/n protocol and supports Station mode, SoftAP mode, SoftAP + Station mode, and promiscuous mode
– A Bluetooth LE subsystem that supports features of Bluetooth 5 and Bluetooth mesh
– 32bit RISCV singlecore processor with a four-stage pipeline that operates at up to 160 MHz
– State-of-the-art power and RF performance

- Storage capacities ensured by 400 KB of SRAM (16 KB for cache) and 384 KB of ROM on the chip, and SPI, Dual SPI, Quad SPI, and QPI interfaces that allow connection to external flash
- Reliable security features ensured by:
  - Cryptographic hardware accelerators that support AES-128/256, Hash, RSA, HMAC, digital signature and secure boot
  - Random number generator
  - Permission control on accessing internal memory, external memory, and peripherals
  - External memory encryption and decryption
- Rich set of peripheral interfaces and GPIOs, ideal for various scenarios and complex applications

Even the lowest-cost connectivity solution needs to provide an appropriate level of security for common security threats. ESP32-C3 is designed to address this threat model.

1. **Secure Boot:** ESP32-C3 implements the standard RSA-3072-based authentication scheme to ensure that only trusted applications can be used on the platform. This feature protects from executing a malicious application programmed in the flash. We understand that secure boot needs to be efficient, so that instant-on devices (such as light bulbs) can take advantage of this feature. ESP32-C3's secure boot implementation adds less than 100ms overhead in the boot process.

2. **Flash Encryption:** ESP32-C3 uses the AES-128-XTS-based flash encryption scheme, whereby the application as well as the configuration data can remain encrypted in the flash. The flash controller supports the execution of encrypted application firmware. Not only does this provide the necessary protection for sensitive data stored in the flash, but it also protects from runtime firmware changes that constitute time-of-check-time-of-use attacks.

3. **Digital Signature and HMAC Peripheral:** ESP32-C3 has a digital signature peripheral that can generate digital signatures, using a private-key that is protected from firmware access. Similarly, the HMAC peripheral can generate a cryptographic digest with a secret that is protected from firmware access. Most of the IoT cloud services use the X.509-certificate-based authentication, and the digital signature peripheral protects the device's private key that defines the device's identity. This provides a strong protection for the device's identity even in case of software vulnerability exploits.

4. **World Controller:** ESP32-C3 has a new peripheral called world controller. This provides two execution environments fully isolated from each other. Depending on the configuration, this can be used to implement a Trusted Execution Environment (TEE) or a privilege separation scheme. If the application firmware has a task that deals with sensitive security data (such as the DRM service), it can take advantage of the world controller and isolate the execution.

Additionally, the proposed solution can be scaled to more complex scenarios by using SBC cluster, see an example in the Fig. 11 taken from [21]. The principles of the development of cluster computing systems based on single-board computers are discussed in [26].

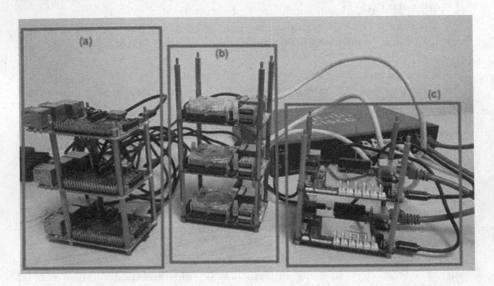

Fig. 11. Example of 3 SBC clusters, devices in each cluster (a, b, c) connect to a Ethernet switch [21].

5 Conclusions and Future Works

The results of this work constitute the foundations for the development of a computing module that can adapt to various key scenarios of the economy and society with a minimum of investment and a maximum of sovereignty. These principles guarantee the sustainability of the main results of this work. The equipment and computer programs that are obtained follow the paradigms of free knowledge, so they will allow their continuous improvement, reuse and evolution towards other scenarios that cannot be addressed by the scope of this work. The electronics industry and the computerization of society could reproduce them on a large scale, which would replace imports, reduce production costs, minimize the impact on the environment and would achieve the linkage with other interested entities with a view to their commercialization. The key sectors of the economy and society (tourism, agriculture, education, health, culture, and others) found in the results of this work a way to achieve their computerization reducing costs and gaining the sovereignty posed in the Sustainable Development Goals of the Agenda 2030 of the United Nations Program for Development. For the continuity of the work it is required to carry out the acquisition of equipment and components that allow testing and adjusting its final development.

References

1. Adnan, A., Tahir, Z., Asis, M.A.: Performance evaluation of single board computer for Hadoop distributed file system (HDFS). In: 2019 International Conference on Information and Communications Technology (ICOIACT), pp. 624–627. IEEE (2019)
2. Al-Sarawi, S., Anbar, M., Abdullah, R., Al Hawari, A.B.: Internet of Things market analysis forecasts, 2020–2030. In: 2020 Fourth World Conference on Smart Trends in Systems, Security and Sustainability (WorldS4), pp. 449–453. IEEE (2020)
3. Ali, F., Yigang, H., Yi, R.: A novel security architecture of internet of things. Int. J. Comput. Theory Eng. **11**(5), 89–96 (2019)
4. Asaithambi, S.P.R., Venkatraman, S., Venkatraman, R.: Big data and personalisation for non-intrusive smart home automation. Big Data Cogn. Comput. **5**(1), 6 (2021)
5. Bourhnane, S., Abid, M.R., Zine-dine, K., Elkamoun, N., Benhaddou, D.: Cluster of single-board computers at the edge for smart grids applications. Appl. Sci. **11**(22), 10981 (2021)
6. Corral-García, J., González-Sánchez, J.L., Pérez-Toledano, M.Á.: Evaluation of strategies for the development of efficient code for Raspberry Pi devices. Sensors **18**(11), 4066 (2018)
7. Cubadebate, R.: En cuba, más cerca de la televisión digital (2021). https://bit.ly/3EyDXYB
8. Díaz-Canel Bermúdez, M.: Why do we need a system of government management system based on science and innovation? Anales de la Academia de Ciencias de Cuba **11**(1) (2021)
9. El-Hajjar, M., Hanzo, L.: A survey of digital television broadcast transmission techniques. IEEE Commun. Surv. Tutor. **15**(4), 1924–1949 (2013). https://doi.org/10.1109/SURV.2013.030713.00220
10. Elsokah, M.M., Saleh, H.H., Ze, A.R.: Next generation home automation system based on voice recognition. In: Proceedings of the 6th International Conference on Engineering & MIS 2020, pp. 1–7 (2020)
11. Fernández-Cerero, D., Fernández-Rodríguez, J.Y., Álvarez-García, J.A., Soria-Morillo, L.M., Fernández-Montes, A.: Single-board-computer clusters for cloudlet computing in internet of things. Sensors **19**(13), 3026 (2019)
12. Figueredo-Reinaldo, O., Carmona-Tamayo, E.: Cuba en datos: Informatización de la sociedad, apuntes más allá de la infraestructura (2021). https://bit.ly/33WIozH
13. Fuzhou Rockchip Electronics Co., L.: Rockchip RK3399 Datasheet (2018)
14. Galkin, P., Golovkina, L., Klyuchnyk, I.: Analysis of single-board computers for IoT and IIoT solutions in embedded control systems. In: 2018 International Scientific-Practical Conference Problems of Infocommunications. Science and Technology (PIC S&T), pp. 297–302. IEEE (2018)
15. Garg, N.: Technology in healthcare: vision of smart hospitals. In: Handbook of Research on Engineering, Business, and Healthcare Applications of Data Science and Analytics, pp. 346–362. IGI Global (2020)
16. Johnston, S.J., Apetroaie-Cristea, M., Scott, M., Cox, S.J.: Applicability of commodity, low cost, single board computers for internet of things devices. In: 2016 IEEE 3rd World Forum on Internet of Things (WF-IoT), pp. 141–146. IEEE (2016)
17. Khanna, A., Kaur, S.: Evolution of internet of things (IoT) and its significant impact in the field of precision agriculture. Comput. Electron. Agric. **157**, 218–231 (2019)

18. Lee, S.K., Bae, M., Kim, H.: Future of IoT networks: a survey. Appl. Sci. **7**(10), 1072 (2017)
19. Manore, C., Manjunath, P., Larkin, D.: Performance of single board computers for vision processing. In: 2021 IEEE 11th Annual Computing and Communication Workshop and Conference (CCWC), pp. 0883–0889. IEEE (2021)
20. Neumann, T.: The single-board computer as a toll to measure the weather parameters in the marine areas. Int. J. Marine Navig. Safety Sea Transp. **14**(4) (2020). https://doi.org/10.12716/1001.14.04.14
21. Qureshi, B., Kawlaq, K., Koubaa, A., Saeed, B., Younis, M.: A commodity SBC-edge cluster for smart cities. In: 2019 2nd International Conference on Computer Applications & Information Security (ICCAIS), pp. 1–6. IEEE (2019)
22. Rico-Bautista, D., Medina-Cárdenas, Y., Guerrero, C.D.: Smart university: a review from the educational and technological view of internet of things. In: Rocha, Á., Ferrás, C., Paredes, M. (eds.) ICITS 2019. AISC, vol. 918, pp. 427–440. Springer, Cham (2019). https://doi.org/10.1007/978-3-030-11890-7_42
23. Systems, E.: ESP32-C3 Series Datasheet (2022). https://www.espressif.com/sites/default/files/documentation/esp32-c3_datasheet_en.pdf
24. Tyagi, H., Patvekar, A.: The concept of smart room in hotels. Int. J. Trend Sci. Res. Dev. **3**, 1314–1318 (2019)
25. UNDP: Sustainable Development Goals Booklet. United Nations Development Programme (2015)
26. Vavrenyuk, A.B., Makarov, V.V., Pryakhin, V.S., Pavlov, M.P., Vasileva, A.A.: Performance evaluation of a cluster computing system running OpenBSD based on single-board computers. In: Misyurin, S.Y., Arakelian, V., Avetisyan, A.I. (eds.) Advanced Technologies in Robotics and Intelligent Systems. MMS, vol. 80, pp. 121–126. Springer, Cham (2020). https://doi.org/10.1007/978-3-030-33491-8_14
27. Whitney, W., et al.: For the 28th consecutive year, Cuba prepares to indict US blockade at united nations. Guardian (Sydney) (1888), 12 (2019)
28. Yadav, V., Mishra, D.K., Singh, P., Tripathi, P.K.: Home automation system using Raspberry Pi Zero W. Int. J. Adv. Intell. Paradigms **16**(2), 216–226 (2020)

A Process for Gathering Data to Train the NLU Module of a NLI System for ITV

Tiffany Marques[1]([⊠]) [ID], Rita Santos[2] [ID], Jorge Abreu[1] [ID], Pedro Beça[1] [ID], Telmo Silva[1] [ID], and Pedro Almeida[1] [ID]

[1] DigiMedia, Department of Communication and Art, University of Aveiro, 3810-193 Aveiro, Portugal
{tiffanymarques,jfa,pedrobeca,tsilva,almeida}@ua.pt

[2] DigiMedia, Águeda School of Technology and Management of Aveiro, University of Aveiro, 3754-909 Aveiro, Portugal
rita.santos@ua.pt

Abstract. The performance of the natural language understanding (NLU) module is a key issue when developing a natural language interaction (NLI) system. For the NLU to perform in an accurate way, it must be trained to correctly understand a wide scope of users' intentions and give (correct) answers. The interaction context must also be considered, meaning that optimizing a NLI system for the TV domain, with a conversational dynamic close to that of humans, involves a complex process capable of gathering a relevant set of natural and diverse utterances for the television specific context. Considering this, the purpose of this paper is to report a process for gathering utterances, which was later be converted into selected data to train the NLU module of a NLI system developed to search a huge number of video content and to control the ever-increasing features of a Smart TV or a Set-Top Box (STB). The process involved real users' data, close monitoring, and active intervention of a support team. The results of the study highlight that integrating easy-to-use feedback mechanisms (WhatsApp and "Flag Failure" buttons embedded in the mobile app), along with the creation of a continuous dynamic with the participants to stimulate their interactions, are paramount to improving the collection of natural and diverse utterances.

Keywords: Natural language understanding · Training data · iTV

1 Introduction

Voice interaction already plays an important role when dealing with the ever-increasing features of advanced interactive TV (iTV) solutions and with the almost endless offer of TV and video content [1]. Nowadays there are commercial solutions, such as LG Voice Mate, Google Assistant, Xfinity, Alexa and Bixby systems, allowing to search for TV content by voice, without having to resort to a more complex interaction via the TV remote control [1]. However, unlike command-based voice interaction systems, where the user interaction is modelled by saying known and limited commands, in a natural language interaction (NLI) system the training and continuous improvement of

© Springer Nature Switzerland AG 2022
M. J. Abásolo and G. F. Olmedo Cifuentes (Eds.): jAUTI 2021, CCIS 1597, pp. 133–147, 2022.
https://doi.org/10.1007/978-3-031-22210-8_9

the natural language understanding (NLU) module are of paramount importance [2]. Tuning this module has the complex challenge of mapping users' phrases to identify their intentions and making them noticeable to the system. The training data collection process, therefore, should be able to gather natural words and phrases, and associate them to each previously identified intent, allowing the recognition of a huge diversity of users' requests [3].

When dealing with the specific iTV domain, a well-trained NLU module should be able to react to situations such as when a user asks for a type of content, even though in an indirect way (e.g., "I'm upset! Show me something to laugh at", "What did the prime minister say today in the news?") or wants a reaction from the system to a statement or a question (e.g., "The sound is too loud!", "Should I take an umbrella tomorrow?"). Although it does not have a direct implication in the training data collection processes, it is worth mentioning that each language has its own syntax, grammar, semantic and linguistic details [4], which prevent for instance a NLI system trained to Brazilian Portuguese to work in a satisfactory way for European Portuguese.

There is no single formula for gathering data for training the NLU module, hence different approaches have been followed by researchers and professionals in the sector. One of the main issues is the fact that collected data is usually not obtained in real contexts [5, 6]. In this way, the main purpose of this paper is to describe the process used under the CHIC project [7], involving the major IPTV provider in Portugal, for the collection of utterances to train the NLU module of a NLI system for the TV domain. This process aims to achieve a wide diversity of possible utterances (relevant to the needs of the users and for their daily interaction with the TV) with the support of users framed in a real context of use. The process used includes the phases of collecting utterances, its organization/analysis, and the final enrichment of the NLU data set by converting the collected utterances into training data. After this introductory section, the paper is structured as follows: Sect. 2 presents the related work on data collection approaches for training NLU modules; the process for gathering training data for the TV lexicon is dealt in Sect. 3; Sect. 4 presents the results and discussion from the process of gathering training data; and the conclusions are presented in Sect. 5.

2 Background

Methods such as crowdsourcing, and Wizard-of-Oz (WoZ) are commonly used to collect data to train NLU modules. Although crowdsourcing has the main advantages of allowing to reach a high number of participants, individuality of people, and reduced costs [5], the breadth of data collected can be limited, as the individuals involved in crowdsourcing generally represent a specific group - typically young people between the ages of 18 and 35 years old with digital knowledge [3]. WoZ, on the other hand, although a useful method for collecting an initial set of data, requires a greater operationalisation effort, since it requires substantial support from specialists [6], as well as some time requirement to test with a large sample. In addition, data collected from both methods may not reflect real utterances [5, 6], as the imaginary performance of tasks do not exactly reflect the real context of using a system.

Training a NLU module using data collected from spontaneous use of the system, in a real context, can be advantageous. Examples of this type of training can be found in academic works, reporting to have successful results. Kapoor & Tirkaz [8], for example, trained the NLU component of a voice assistant in German in two phases. First, the researchers did a focused training, with activities aimed at a smaller group of participants. With this first phase, the researchers were able to evaluate the model developed. Next, the researchers collected data from spontaneous use of the system. This way, they managed to obtain a greater variety of phrases.

To increase the participation of users in the creation of the training data, it is still possible to use additional incentive mechanisms within the gathering process. Such an approach is usually based on a crowdsourcing contest, which incorporates concepts based on tournaments and auctions [9]. Generally, participants receive challenges, which can yield some type of reward [10]. To encourage the participation of crowd workers, Hettiachchi et al. [11] offered US$20 vouchers to those who have interacted the most with the proposed challenges. According to the researchers, the stimulus boosted the number of interactions in the study, which aimed to measure the performance of tasks using a regular graphical interface versus digital voice assistants. The results of the study showed that the researchers obtained satisfactory quality data. In this sense, it is believed that contests can be quick and direct mechanisms to obtain greater involvement as reported by [12].

In the commercial context, companies exploring conversational artificial intelligence (AI) are also looking into the best approaches to collect data, and even designing processes around that goal, as is the case of Rasa,[1] a company dedicated to developing a standard infrastructure for conversational AI [13]. According to Rasa documentation [14] the process of gathering training data should have conversation-driven development (CDD) in mind. CDD, through a set of activities and principles, allows to guide the decisions of a development team, in the creation and improvement of the assistant, to correctly meet the users' requests. To this end, it envisages collecting real data from user interactions, namely in an uncontrolled environment as a Field Trial (which enables a greater naturalness in user interactions), which allows for better performance of the NLU module. This approach is, thus, different from text generation tools or models which, despite generating many synthetic training data, do not really represent user interactions [14], as they do not reflect a real interaction context. CDD comprises six steps: 1) Share - test the prototype at an early stage of the development process with users not belonging to the development team; 2) Review - analyse the training data of the interaction between the users and the assistant; 3) Annotate - convert the data into examples for training; 4) Test - perform tests whenever updates are made to the assistant; 5) Track - use meaningful metrics (e.g.: frequency of most common assistant actions and most commonly used terms) to have a greater understanding of what is working correctly and incorrectly; 6) Fix - continually carry out adjustments (based on the analysis of user interactions with the assistant) to reduce failures in the long term. This process, besides being user-centered, is iterative, which allows a continuous improvement of the assistant and its potentialities. Moreover, the various steps can be carried out simultaneously [15].

There are many specificities inherent to the TV domain, especially when OTT (Over the Top) content and other devices come into stake. The number of on-demand content platforms, such as Netflix or Disney+, is growing, a feature that goes against the linear

---

[1] https://rasa.com.

visualization of programs [16]. The TV-set (either a regular TV connected to a STB or a Smart TV) can even be used as a personal information aggregator, since it can display useful data for everyday life, such as traffic or weather conditions. In addition, the user can, for example, browse through a variety of applications like those installed in one's smartphone.

Aiming to identify studies related to collecting training data approaches for the NLU module considering the television lexicon, a thorough research was done on different platforms (Mendeley, Scopus, Google Scholar, ACM Digital Library and IEEE Xplore). Search sentences, such as "TV training AND NLU", "TV training data", "TV training AND television" and "television OR data training", were used (last accessed 2021/9/10). Unfortunately, no relevant results were found as, probably, NLU training tends to be developed by major industry players, who do not usually share their strategies on the topic.

3 Process for Gathering Training Data for NLI System

As part of the CHIC project [7], it was intended to develop a NLI system for both navigation and content search (in the context of an IPTV service) using European Portuguese semantics. As the performance of the NLI system relies on a continuous improvement approach, to ensure a good efficiency of the NLU module an iterative process was followed, gathering natural and diversified utterances for the different intents of the TV lexicon, and identifying and solving problems in an agile way.

In this context, the collection of utterances for training the used NLU module (Rasa NLU module supported by BotSchool proprietary technology, which allows to create assistants and have a more user-friendly interface to teach the NLU module [17]) was organised in two phases (Fig. 1). The initial phase of gathering utterances, aimed to overcome the "cold start" of the system, was based on the provision of different types of visual stimuli related with frequent users' actions in the iTV context [18]: **Channels browsing** - search for a channel by name; **TV content search** - search for content by title/name, thematic and trends (popular TV shows); search for channels by thematic; **Automatic TV-recordings** (Catch-up TV service) - access to the latest content of each channel; **Navigation** - access to the TV Guide (EPG), Set-Top Box (STB) menus, programme information and continue watching list; **Video Club** - see rented content; **Apps**

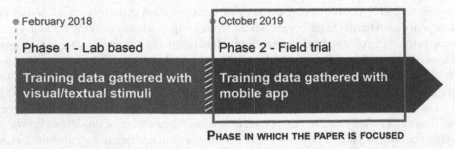

Fig. 1. Phases of gathering training data

- search for apps by thematic or by their name/title; **YouTube** - search for content on the YouTube TV app by name/title or pre-existing category (e.g.: recent videos).

The outputs of this first phase of gathering utterances were fundamental to inform and provide data to the initial training process of the NLU module of the functional prototype developed. This prototype relied on a mobile app from which the Natural Language Interaction is performed[2] in association with an iTV app responsible for displaying the output results to the users (Fig. 2).

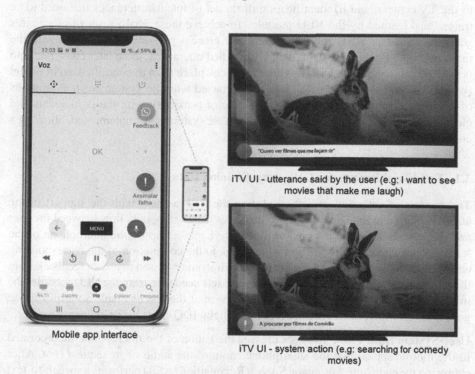

Mobile app interface

iTV UI - utterance said by the user (e.g: I want to see movies that make me laugh)

iTV UI - system action (e.g: searching for comedy movies)

Fig. 2. Prototype of the NLI system for iTV

To increase the naturalness of users' interactions with the system, alternative decoys were created for textual feedbacks, which expressed a more empathetic and user-friendly tone, such as: "The virtual command has an OK button which is easier to use!:)", "Unfortunately I can't do it yet...: (But soon I will" and "Unfortunately I couldn't find what you were looking for: (" and, eleven copywriting quotes, like "Hello!:) How can I help you" and "See you next time!:)" to standardise the discourse of the system.

A set of novelty phrases has also been programmed so that the system reacts to user's jokes/prompts. For example, if users made requests like "Tell me a joke" or "I'm a little late. What's the best route to work?", the system will give answers like "Okay... Have you ever heard of the claustrophobic astronaut? He just needed a little bit of space!: D" and "I thought so...:) Unfortunately, I still can't do it...", respectively. These examples

---

[2] Due to technical restrictions of the commercial STB used by the IPTV provider, the integration of the NLI feature in this already existent app was the best trade-off to support this research.

do not refer to possible actions specifically related to the TV context, however, have the potential to lead to a more natural and empathetic use of the system.

In the second phase (Fig. 1), a more complete utterance collection process was carried out in a Field Trial (FT), which allowed to test the prototype in real conditions and thus to collect a greater number of diverse and natural utterances. This paper focuses on this second phase of gathering training utterances, in which the following aims were defined: i) collection of more diversified and natural utterances for the different intents related to the TV context; and ii) identification of the set of intents/utterances that need to be trained and learned by the NLU module. To achieve these goals, a set of procedures was established in a FT, following the CDD process previously described, with the main purpose of collecting natural and diversified utterances, to be later converted into organized data to train the NLU module. As it took place in an uncontrolled environment (where the conditions under which users interacted with the system, such as in terms of noise, could not be controlled), a dynamic of proximity with the participants and close monitoring of the user's interaction with the system was implemented, allowing a continuous improvement of the system.

3.1 Field Trial Process for Collecting Training Data

The process of gathering utterances during the FT was held with the support of the already referred mobile app. Figure 3 illustrates the existing data flow between the user and the system, from the moment an utterance is picked up by the microphone of the smartphone, where the mobile app is installed, to the completion of the corresponding action in the STB. Figure 3 also reflects all the instruments used to obtain feedback from the participants and the respective training datasets needed to train the NLU module (the infographic here presented is a simplified version of the one available at: https://drive.google.com/drive/folders/1fnO84rWNU9fTajhgbwJDQ1BGa4d8BC-F?usp=sharing).

User-System Data Flow. The user presses the button of the microphone incorporated in the mobile app so that the smartphone captures the audio of its request (1^3). After capturing the audio, the Automatic Speech Recognition (ASR) performs a speech-to-text conversion of the user's request (2). This conversion generates a text file that is processed and stored in the cloud. Subsequently, the request converted to text is sent to the mobile app (3), communicated to the iTV/STB app (4) and displayed on the iTV UI (5). The utterance processed by the ASR is transmitted as the user interacts in natural language with the system (in real time).

For the system to perform an action, the mobile app sends the text converted by the ASR to an API (6), where all the elements, allowing the various components of the solution to be articulated, are implemented. From there, it goes to the BotSchool, where the interpretation and conversion of text into commands occurs (7). Once the conversion is done, the command is returned, via the API (8), to the mobile app (9) that will transmit it to the App-TV/STB (10). Finally, the interpreted intent and corresponding results are displayed in the UI (11).

---

[3] Each number represents a stage of the user-system data flow, shown in Fig. 3.

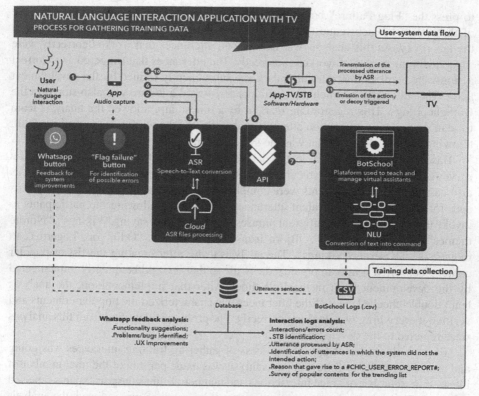

Fig. 3. Infographic of the process for gathering training data

If there is a misinterpretation of the utterance by the NLU, two possible actions may occur, either the system performs an action that is not as expected or issues a decoy, such as "Sorry, I still can't help you with what you asked for".

Managing the Process of the Field Trial. To carry out the FT, a daily dynamic of gathering, organizing and analysing data was followed. As the gathering of utterances took place in a real and not controlled context, it was necessary to design a strategy to record all participants' interactions and to allow them to give feedback when the system did not react to something as they wanted. To achieve this, two dedicated buttons were implemented in the app: a) a red button to flag errors and utterances not correctly interpreted ("Flag Failure" button shown in Fig. 3); and b) a green button acting as a shortcut to a dedicated WhatsApp channel allowing users to text or send an audio/video message addressing the reported errors and suggestions for improving the system (WhatsApp button shown in Fig. 3).

Daily, the BotSchool logs (written in.csv files) were downloaded and exported to a dedicated database. The exported data allowed a daily analysis of the logs of all the interactions reaching the NLU, namely the NLU outputs of the participants' interactions with the system, identification of the STB used, iTV text outputs as responses to user-system interactions, correspondent triggered actions, and reasons that led the participants to press the "Flag Failure" button. The analysis team was able to verify the response of the system to each request of the user (sentence) by replicating those requests in the laboratory. As this analysis was carried out, utterances that worked correctly were separated from those that worked incorrectly. The utterances that triggered an incorrect action were converted into training data and subsequently trained by the development team. The situations in which the participants reported a failure was also stored in the BotSchool logs. This registration, marked by a timestamp, allowed the analysis team to scan the previous interaction attempts that motivated the participant to report a fault, allowing them to identify what was the system error.

Based on the data present in the database from the BotSchool's daily.csv files, a survey of popular TV content (recurring and seasonal TV programs of high audience) was also carried out. These contents were compiled to create a list of popular TV programs and, for each of them, equivalent utterances were defined allowing the participants to invoke those contents using different phrases as, for example, saying "Vikings", "Nordic themes", "Ragnar Lothbrok", "Bjorn Ironside", "Valhalla", "Odin" or "Lagertha" to request the TV series "Vikings". The analysis team, after creating the list of popular content, converted it into an organized.csv file so that it could be directly implemented by the development team in the BotSchool. After that implementation, the analysis team double-checked each of the utterances that characterized the popular contents and verified if everything was working correctly. The problems identified from this analysis were reported to the development team.

To get a clear idea of how the process of gathering training utterances was going and to make it easier to follow up, an analysis was made per day of the total number of interactions (number of voice interactions and number of times the participants reported a failure). Thus, on the days when the number of interactions was reduced, the analysis team could remember the participants of the importance to use the system to improve it. An analysis of the number of utterances associated with each intent was also made.

In addition to the analysis of the daily.csv files, feedback obtained from the participants via WhatsApp was also screened to identify problems/bugs, suggestions for new features or UX improvements. After that, the analysis team informed the development team about the issues that should be tackled. To reinforce the importance of the participants' contribution, all improvements/corrections implemented in the system were informed by e-mail on a regular basis.

As a way of boosting the process of gathering and creating training utterances, a set of initiatives have been developed to create a closer dynamic with the participants and thus encourage the continued use of the NLI system. Periodic communications of the improvements introduced, awarding prizes to the most active participants, and sending out challenges (2 per week) were the initiatives developed for this purpose. The challenges were planned to introduce new or improved functionalities, or with the objective of collecting diverse and natural utterances for the less used commands, such as asking the participants to search the latest results of the SL Benfica games, using the Sports TV app. In the case of the challenges two e-mails were sent: one with the challenge and another one with some examples of utterances (trained prior to the challenge) that could be used to actions related to the challenge.

3.2 Summary of the Operationalization Process

In summary, Table 1 presents the operationalization of the CDD process used during the FT for gathering the training data. This operationalization is divided into the six steps that comprise the CDD process (share, review, annotate, track, fix and test).

Table 1. Operationalization of the CDD process in our work

CDD steps	CDD process	Operationalization process
Share	Test the prototype at an early stage of the development process with users outside the development team	Participants external to the analysis and development team tested the NLI system, in a real context of use (FT)
Review	Analyse the training data of the interaction between user and assistant	Daily analysis of the interaction logs, from the CSVs provided by the BotSchool
Annotate	Convert the data into examples for training	Utterances spoken by users that triggered incorrect actions due to a lack of language comprehension were converted into training data. This was also the case in situations where participants flagged a "failure" due to NLU limitations/faults. Alternative utterances were created for users requesting popular content were also converted into training data
Track	Use meaningful metrics to have a greater understanding of what is working correctly and incorrectly	For the analysis team to have a greater understanding of the performance of the system, an analysis was made of the: • daily number of voice interactions; • daily number of participants who pressed the "Flag failure" button; • number of interactions from the challenges; • total number of utterances collected per intent and action; • number of incorrect actions to participants' requests. An analysis was also made of the feedbacks given by the participants via WhatsApp
Fix	Continually carry out adjustments to reduce failures in the long term	The development team used BotSchool technology to train the NLU module, fix issues/bugs detected by the participants and analysis team, and implement and improve features
Test	Perform tests whenever updates are made to the assistant	Testing was carried out throughout the FT period. When the development team updated the system, emails were sent to the participants mentioning the implemented improvements

4   Results

4.1 Participants' Characterization

29 participants were engaged in the FT, where 22 participants (75.9%) were male and 7 (24.1%) female. Based on a convenience sample, two criteria were used to choose the participants: their digital literacy and prior knowledge of iTV apps. Regarding age, there was a great variety, since the youngest user was 22 years old and the oldest 78.

The average was 43 years. The most representative age ranges were 35–39 years (7) and 42–46 years (7). Regarding the education level, 48.3% had a bachelor's or undergraduate degree; 44.8% a master's degree; and 3.4% PhD, the same number of participants who indicated that they had secondary education.

Television is a device often used by participants: 82.8% indicated that they watch some type of program at least once a day. The average daily time devoted to television consumption was 2 h 45 min. Concerning virtual assistants (e.g., Google Home, Amazon Echo), these devices are the least used by participants (51,7% of respondents said they never had contact with this technology), compared to TVs, smart TVs, smartphones (to control TV) and media players.

4.2 Collection of Diversified and Natural Utterances

The process of gathering utterances, during the FT, took place between October 2019 and April 2020 (totalling 169 days). The interaction logs showed that a total of 5194 interactions occurred throughout the FT, where 4777 corresponded to voice interactions and 417 corresponded to the number of times the participants pressed the "Flag failure" button. For this total number of interactions (coming from all participants), it took, on average, approximately 4 h of work per day from a member of the analysis team were required to perform the analysis of the training data gathered.

Despite the high number of interactions in the first few days (243 interactions on the 1st day of the FT), throughout the FT this number decreased stabilising at a daily average of 15 interactions. At the beginning of the 2nd stage of the FT, the number of interactions remained low. So, as of 12 February 2020, challenges were presented to the participants (2 per week) to increase the daily average of interactions and make the process of gathering training utterances more dynamic. As a result, the number of interactions increased significantly. For example, at the launch of the 1st challenge – "Try content reproduction controls", 354 interactions were obtained. However, it should be noted that the interactions arising from the 1st challenge do not exactly reflect the number of interactions of the remaining challenges, as the average number of interactions arising from the challenges was 79. The peaks seen in Fig. 4, as of 12 February 2020, resulted from the days when challenges were sent.

Regarding the number of utterances collected per intent, Table 2 shows that "TV Content Search/YouTube" (1947) and "Navigation" (1279) represented 67,53% of the requests made by participants. The "Automatic TV-Recordings" was the intent which obtained the least utterances (77). When analysing by action name[4] and not by intent, the lowest number of utterances was obtained in searchGambling (search of euromillion results) (1) and searchLiveContent (2) from the intents Apps/Videoclub and TV Content Search/YouTube, respectively.

---

[4] Refers to the action triggered by the NLI system. Each intent may have several associated actions names.

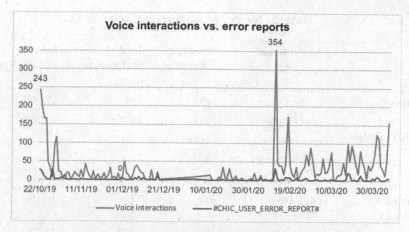

Fig. 4. Voice interactions counting and error reports

Trained Utterances/Intents. To confirm whether the utterances spoken by the participants triggered the right actions, the analysis team carried out daily laboratory tests in
which the requests made by the participants were reproduced. From these tests, it was
verified the existence of 423 utterances (8,85%) that did not act in accordance with the
requests made by the participants and, consequently, needed further training. In the 3rd
phase (the last phase of the process), 129 utterances were trained. The remaining utterances represented pending problems (254), not applicable (38) or impossible to perform
(2). The pending problems were related to functionalities that were not available at the
time of the user-system interaction, but were foreseen to be implemented, such as the
utterances that refer to the commands "Restart" and "Maximum/Minimum Volume".

When testing the utterances which motivated participants to press the "Flag failure"
button (interaction prior to an error), it was perceived that too vague commands (14), nonexistent (16) or foreseen functionalities (88), system down by server updates (61), and
content unavailable in the iTV catalogue (31) were the main reasons that led participants
to report failures.

The daily analysis made to the interaction logs enabled not only greater agility in
the detection of utterances that did not correctly execute the intended actions but also
the quick tracking of the main reasons that led the participants to report a failure. The
main advantage of the "Flag failure" button focuses on the fact that, with just one click,
participants could report the existence of a problem without having to describe it, which
resulted in a less user-system interaction effort.

The feedback given by the participants using the "WhatsApp" button allowed the
identification of 53 errors. Examples of feedback messages were: "The message perceived by the system does not appear on TV" (P.4[5]); "Searching "You on TV" by voice
leads to the action "to turn off"" (P.15); "The utterance "Turn off the box" translates
into the action "to exit" (P.21); and "The utterance "restart program" does not lead to
any action, nor does generate any feedback" (P.1). Of the errors identified, 37 have been

---

[5] "P.4" represents participant #4.

Table 2. Number of utterances per intent

Intent	Action Name	Counting utterances	Total of utterances per intent	Relative frequency per intent
Channels Browsing	changeChannel	853	853	17,86%
TV Content Search/YouTube	searchByGenre	207	1947	40,76%
	searchByName	1688		
	searchChannel	50		
	searchLiveContent	2		
Automatic TV-Recordings	openGAs	77	77	1,61%
Navigation	continueWatching	79	1279	26,77%
	exitToTV	169		
	Help	20		
	remoteKey	470		
	showText	8		
	tvPause	6		
	tvPlay	15		
	tvRestartContent	14		
	tvShowPit	10		
	volume	488		
Apps/Videoclub	changeRadio	75	621	13%
	openApp	417		
	searchApp	81		
	searchGambling	1		
	searchSoccer	25		
	showWifiPassword	22		

resolved, whereas 16 were not possible to be solved due to technical constraints such as lack of metadata information (e.g. year; and casting).

Training Popular Contents. From the analysis made to the daily .csv files from the BotSchool it was possible to identify 70 popular contents, in which 39 were trained using equivalent utterances that characterize the correspondent trending TV programmes. For example, for the popular content "Batman" utterances like, "Bruce Wayne", "Gotham" and "Dark Knight" have been created as alternatives to request this movie. Due to constant changes in the TV catalogue, contents identified as seasonal (25), which were not available in the catalogue at the time of the analysis, were not trained. The popular content identified and the creation of equivalent utterances that characterize these contents contributed to participants interacting more naturally with the system and being able to find the contents, even without knowing their title/name.

5   Conclusions

The development of a NLI system for the television context requires a deep knowledge of the possible intentions of the user, so that the system is trained to meet their requests, because while humans can naturally assimilate speech, machines are not capable of doing that. Only with a good performance of the NLU, a NLI system can process and understand the meaning of the speech and thus determine the intended action to respond to the user's intention. Considering this, for training the NLU module adapted to the television lexicon, the CDD process was operationalized, in a FT, which allows, in an iterative way to collect a substantial number of diversified and natural utterances and to detect and solve problems/bugs more quickly and efficiently.

The process used to collect training data requires the use of two instruments: the feedback mechanisms "WhatsApp" and "Flag failure" buttons (integrated in the mobile app interface where the NLI takes place), and the BotSchool that makes available daily and automatically.csv files where user interaction records are registered. While the "WhatsApp" button allowed the collection of feedback from participants about problems/bugs they have identified and suggestions for possible improvements, the "Flag Failure" button enabled the user to quickly report an error with just one click. Without this feedback mechanism training would be much more difficult, as it would not be clear whether the statements referred to actions were correctly or incorrectly interpreted. The.csv files from the BotSchool, after their treatment and analysis, allowed the collection and training of diverse and natural utterances for the different intents of the television lexicon. From it, it was also possible to identify: utterances that do not meet the expectations of the users and therefore need to be trained; content trends; and main reasons that led participants to flag failures.

The designed dynamics enabled not only greater efficiency in processing and analysing data from the used instruments, but also greater proximity between participants and the teams involved in the study (analysis and development teams). Sending the improvements made to the system, providing feedback from the analysis team in response to what participants reported via WhatsApp, launching challenges, and delivering awards (extrinsic motivator) to the most active participants contributed to the streamlining of the dynamics, as well as to give participants a perception that the NLI system was continuously being improved. In addition, to help make the speech more cordial, friendly and empathetic between the user and the system, decoys, copywriting suggestions and novelty phrases were created.

Although the need for an active team to support the process described of gathering data to train the NLU module, the process has made the system more capable of responding to users' requests. It also revealed to be very important to respond quickly and efficiently to the problems detected by the users and to permanently have a good performance of the NLU. This is especially relevant when the TV catalogue is updated with new and trending TV programs.

Faced with a need for continuous improvement of the NLI system, namely its functionalities and the NLU module, in the next phase of the project (pilot), it is intended to continue gathering data to train the system to make the user experience more natural. Using contextual information, it is intended to implement some conversational use-cases. Providing the system with functionalities such as fine content selection, disambiguation of requests and content suggestion in response to certain conversational user interactions is a following step in that direction.

In the pilot, using the same NLI system, it is also intended to understand how the overall user experience will be affected if the voice input is supported via a TV remote control with an integrated microphone. To achieve this, a dedicated technical setup is being implemented enabling the analysis team to study the preferences of the users regarding the voice input device.

Acknowledgments. This paper is a result of the project CHIC - Cooperative Holistic View on Internet and Content (grant agreement number 24498), funded by COMPETE 2020 and Portugal 2020 through the European Regional Development Fund (FEDER).

References

1. Ferraz de Abreu, J., Santos, R., Silva, T., Marques, T., Cardoso, B.: Proactivity: the next step in voice assistants for the TV ecosystem. In: Abásolo, M.J., Kulesza, R., Pina Amargós, J.D. (eds.) jAUTI 2019. CCIS, vol. 1202, pp. 103–116. Springer, Cham (2020). https://doi.org/10.1007/978-3-030-56574-9_7
2. Braun, D., Mendez, A.H., Matthes, F., Langen, M.: Evaluating natural language understanding services for conversational question answering systems. In: Proceedings of the 18th Annual SIGdial Meeting on Discourse and Dialogue, Saarbrücken, pp. 174–185. ACL (2017)
3. Braunger, P., Maier, W., Wessling, J., Schmidt, M.: Towards an automatic assessment of crowdsourced data for NLU. In: Proceedings of the Eleventh International Conference on Language Resources and Evaluation, ELRA (2018)
4. Ali, A., Magdy, W., Renals, S.: Multi-reference evaluation for dialectal speech recognition system: a study for Egyptian ASR. In: Proceedings of the Second Workshop on Arabic Natural Language Processing, Beijing, China, pp. 118–126. ACL (2015)
5. Eskenazi, M., Levow, G.-A., Meng, H., Parent, G., Suendermann, D.: Crowdsourcing for Speech Processing: Applications to Data Collection, Transcription and Assessment. Wiley, Hoboken (2013)
6. Morbini, F., Forbell, E., Sagae, K.: Improving classification-based natural language understanding with non-expert annotation. In: Proceedings of the 15th Annual Meeting of the Special Interest Group on Discourse and Dialogue, pp. 69–73, Philadelphia. ACL (2014)
7. CHIC: https://chic.mog-technologies.com/. Accessed 31 Oct 2021
8. Kapoor, S., Tirkaz, C.: Bootstrapping NLU models with multi-task learning. In: Computation and Language (2019)
9. Lee, H.C.B., Ba, S., Li, X., Stallaert, J.: Salience bias in crowdsourcing contests. Inf. Syst. Res. **29**(2), 401–418 (2018)
10. Vaughan, J.: Making better use of the crowd: how crowdsourcing can advance machine learning research. J. Mach. Learn. Res. **18**(193), 1–46 (2018)
11. Hettiachchi, D., et al.: "Hi! I am the Crowd Tasker" crowdsourcing through digital voice assistants. In: Proceedings of the 2020 CHI Conference on Human Factors in Computing Systems (CHI 2020), pp. 1–14. ACM, New York (2020)
12. Chawla, S., Hartline, J.D., Sivan, B.: Optimal crowdsourcing contests. Games Econ. Behav. **113**, 80–96 (2019)

13. Rasa: https://rasa.com/about/. Accessed 31 Oct 2021
14. Rasa Docs: Generating NLU Data. https://rasa.com/docs/rasa/generating-nlu-data. Accessed 15 Oct 2021
15. Rasa: The CDD Playbook. https://info.rasa.com/cdd-playbook. Accessed 15 Oct 2021
16. McNally, J., Diederich, E.: Browsing for content across pay TV and on demand video options. In: Proceedings of the 2019 ACM International Conference on Interactive Experiences for TV and Online Video (TVX 2019), pp. 129–136. ACM Press, New York (2019)
17. AlticeLabs: A better way to create intelligent virtual assistant. https://www.alticelabs.com/content/WP_BOTSchool.pdf. Accessed 15 Oct 2021
18. Santos, R., Ferraz de Abreu, J., Almeida, P., Beça, P., Marques, T.: Training natural language understanding for the TV context: a visual stimuli approach for the elicitation process. In: Abásolo, M.J., Kulesza, R., Pina Amargós, J.D. (eds.) jAUTI 2019. CCIS, vol. 1202, pp. 89–102. Springer, Cham (2020). https://doi.org/10.1007/978-3-030-56574-9_6

Author Index

Printed in the United States
by Baker & Taylor Publisher Services